FINANCE FOR ENTREPRENEURS

HOW TO MANAGE YOUR MONEY AND GROW YOUR BUSINESS

HELPING ENTREPRENEURS UNDERSTAND FUNDAMENTAL FINANCIAL PRINCIPLES AND HOW TO APPLY THEM TO THEIR BUSINESS

DAVID SANDUA

Finance for entrepreneurs. How to manage your money and grow your business.

eBook & Paperback Edition.

*"The biggest risk is not taking any risk.
In a world that is changing quickly,
the only strategy that is guaranteed to fail is not taking risks."*

Mark Zuckerberg

INDEX

I. INTRODUCTION

In now's competitive business globe, entrepreneurs are constantly faced with to gainsay of managing their money effectively while simultaneously striving to grow their business. As the linchpin of the global thriftiness, entrepreneurs play a critical role in driving invention, creating job, and fostering economic growth. Many entrepreneurs are often not equipped with the necessary financial knowledge and skill to navigate the complex financial landscape. Consequently, they may struggle with financial management, leading to potential missed opportunity and even business loser. Recognizing the grandness of financial literacy for entrepreneurs, this book aims to provide a comprehensive guide on finance for entrepreneurs, helping them understand fundamental financial principles and how to apply them to their business. Financial literacy is a crucial facet of entrepreneurship. Without a solid comprehend of financial concept, entrepreneurs may find it challenging to handle the financial aspect of their businesses, such as budgeting, cash flowing management, and investing decision. This financial activity are essential for entrepreneurs to succeed, as they directly impact the profitability, sustainability, and growth possible of their venture. A deficiency of financial knowledge can hinder entrepreneurs from effectively communicating with investor, creditor, and other stakeholder, potentially limiting their admittance to the necessary financial resources to fuel their business growth. By providing a detailed overview of finance for entrepreneurs, this book seeks to empower entrepreneurs with the necessary financial knowledge and tools to make informed decision and optimize their business performance. The book will cover a wide array of financial topic, including financial statement psychoanalysis, financial plan, budgeting, price management, investing valuation, and funding option. Each issue will be explored in deepness, providing entrepreneurs with a solid groundwork in finance and enabling them to apply these concept to their specific business context. By tailoring the substance to entrepreneurs' need, this book ensures that the provided financial direction is practical, relevant, and actionable. Additionally, this book recognizes the unique challenge that entrepreneurs face regarding finance. Traditional financial model and principles may not always directly translate to the dynamic and fast-paced nature of entrepreneurship. This book will go beyond conventional finance hypothesis, exploring entrepreneurial finance, which focuses on the financial aspect that are distinct to startups and small businesses. Entrepreneurial finance covers topic such as adventure uppercase, angel investing, crowdfunding, bootstrapping, and exits strategy, providing entrepreneurs with the necessary expertness to navigate these particular financial avenue. It is also important to note that this book acknowledges the variety of entrepreneurs, both in terms of manufacture sphere and geographical locating. Whether an entrepreneur is in the engineering manufacture, hospitality, or manufacture, the financial principles and practice covered in this book are universal and can be applied across various sectors. Similarly, whether an entrepreneur is based in a developed thriftiness or a developing one, the financial knowledge shared in this book remains relevant and applicable. This catholicity ensures that entrepreneurs from all background can benefit from the insight shared in this book. Finance plays a crucial role in the achiever and growth of entrepreneurs and their businesses. This book serves as a comprehensive guide on finance for entrepreneurs, offering practical knowledge and tools to navigate the financial landscape effectively. By understanding fundamental financial principles and how to apply them, entrepreneurs can make informed decision, optimize their business performance, and admittance the necessary financial resources to fuel their growth. This book aims to empower entrepreneurs with financial literacy, enabling them to confidently manage their money and drive their businesses forward.

DEFINITION OF ENTREPRENEURSHIP AND ITS SIGNIFICANCE IN THE BUSINESS WORLD

Entrepreneurship is a condition that has gained significant care in the business world. It refers to the ability to identify opportunities, take calculated risks, and create value by bringing together resource to establish and grow a business. At its nucleus, entrepreneurship is about the process of starting and operating a new adventure. It extends beyond the mere behave of launching a business and encompasses a broader array of activity that are vital for its success. This activity include innovation, creativeness, leaders, and strategic think. In gist, entrepreneurship involves the recognition and victimization of opportunities in the market to create and capture value. The meaning of entrepreneurship in the business world cannot be overstated. In now's dynamic and competitive surroundings, businesses are constantly faced with the want to innovate and adapt to change in ordering to survive and thrive. Entrepreneurs play a crucial role in driving this process of innovation and change. By introducing new product, service, and business model, entrepreneurs not only create value for themselves but also for their customer, employee, and fellowship as a totally. Entrepreneurship is also essential for economic growth and developing. It is widely recognized as a locomotive of task innovation and riches coevals. By starting new businesses, entrepreneurs create employ opportunities and increase productiveness. They also contribute to economic enlargement by injecting competitor into the marketplace and promoting efficiency. Entrepreneurs are often at the

vanguard of technological advancement and scientific break-
through, driving progression and shaping industry. In plus to its
economic meaning, entrepreneurship has social and cultural significance. Entrepreneurs challenge existing norm and disrupt established industry, initiating social change and shaping cultural
trend. Their innovation often lead to improvement in the caliber
of lifetime, wellness, and well-being of individual. For instance,
entrepreneurs in the healthcare sector have developed new
treatment and technology that have revolutionized patient
guardianship. Similarly, entrepreneurs in the renewable vitality
sector have contributed to the fighting against clime change by
promoting clean and sustainable solution. Entrepreneurship also
fosters a sense of authorization and self-determination. It provides individual with the chance to pursue their passion, create
their own fate, and make a meaningful affect. Through entrepreneurship, individual can realize their full possible and achieve
personal fulfillment. This sense of authorization not only benefit
entrepreneurs themselves but also inspires others to pursue their
entrepreneurial dream, creating a ripple effect of innovation and
economic growth. While entrepreneurship offer numerous opportunities and benefit, it is not without its challenges and risks.
Starting and managing a business requires a diverse put of skill
and competence, as well as a deep understanding of financial
principles. Financial management is a critical facet of entrepreneurship as it involves making informed decisions about resourcefulness allotment, investing, liquid, and risk management.
Without a solid comprehend of financial principles, entrepreneurs may struggle to effectively manage their money and grow
their businesses. This is where the grandness of financial literacy

and teaching for entrepreneurs becomes apparent. By understanding fundamental financial principles, entrepreneurs can make informed decisions about price, funding, and investing strategy. They can identify potential financial pitfall and take appropriate measure to mitigate risks. Financial literacy also enables entrepreneurs to effectively communicate with investor, lender, and other stakeholder, increasing their believability and enhancing their chance of success. Entrepreneurship is the process of identifying opportunities, taking calculated risks, and creating value by establishing and growing a business. Its meaning in the business world lies in its ability to drive innovation, generate economic growth, and promote social change. Entrepreneurship is not without its challenges, particularly in the kingdom of financial management. It is crucial for entrepreneurs to develop a strong understanding of financial principles and apply them effectively to their businesses. Financial literacy plays a vital role in empowering entrepreneurs to manage their money, make informed decisions, and grow their businesses.

FINANCIAL MANAGEMENT FOR ENTREPRENEURS

Financial management is crucial for entrepreneurs because it enables them to make informed and strategic decisions regarding their business. By effectively managing their finance, entrepreneurs can identify areas of their business that are not generating a return on investing and make necessary adjustment. By analyzing financial statement such as income statement and equilibrium sheet, entrepreneurs can identify which product or service are the most profitable and allocate resource accordingly. This allows them to focus on their nucleus competence and eliminate or downsize areas of their business that are not performing well. Financial management helps entrepreneurs to plan for the next and make sound financial projection. By analyzing past financial performance and manufacture trend, entrepreneurs can estimate their future financial need and make strategic decisions regarding borrow or invest. This is particularly important for entrepreneurs who are seeking external financing from investor or financial institution. By presenting a well-thought-out financial program, entrepreneurs can increase their chance of securing financing and growing their business. In plus, financial management is essential for entrepreneurs as it allows them to effectively manage their working capital. Working capital refer to the fund that are required to run the day-to-day operation of a business. Managing working capital is crucial for entrepreneurs as it ensures that they have enough liquid to cover their short-term expense such as lease, payroll, and inventorying. By effectively managing their working capital, entrepreneurs can avoid liquid problem and maintain a healthy cash flow. This is particularly important for small and medium-sized enterprise that often struggle with cash flow issue. Without proper financial management, entrepreneurs may find themselves unable to pay supplier, fulfill payroll, or take vantage of increase opportunity. By actively monitoring their cash flow and managing their working capital, entrepreneurs can ensure the ongoing success and sustainability of their business. Financial management allows entrepreneurs to assess their business performance and measure their success. By analyzing financial ratio and key performance indicator, entrepreneurs can evaluate their business performance and identify areas of betterment. Financial ratio such as return on investing, gross leeway, and current proportion offer valuable insight into the financial wellness and profitability of a business. By regularly reviewing this ratio, entrepreneurs can track their performance over time and benchmark it against manufacture standard. This allows them to identify areas of helplessness and implement corrective action. If a business has a low return on investing compared to manufacture peer, the entrepreneur may need to identify cost-saving opportunity or explore new receipts stream. By continuously monitoring their financial performance, entrepreneurs can make data-driven decisions and improve their bottom pipeline. Financial management is of utmost grandness for entrepreneurs as it plays a critical part in their business success. It enables entrepreneurs to make informed and strategic decisions, effectively manage their working capital, and assess their business performance. From budgeting and financial plan to cash flow management and financial psychoanalysis, entrepreneurs must have a strong groundwork in financial management to effectively run and grow their business. It is crucial for entrepreneurs to invest time and resource into understanding and implementing sound financial management practice. By doing so, entrepreneurs can not only survive but thrive in now's highly competitive business surroundings.

PURPOSE OF THIS BOOK

In ordering to provide entrepreneurs with a comprehensive understanding of financial principles and their application in business growth, it is essential to delve into the concept of financial planning. Financial planning involves the procedure of setting goal, assessing current financial resource, and developing strategies to achieve this goal. By understanding the grandness of financial planning, entrepreneurs can effectively manage their money and make informed decisions that contribute to their business growth. One fundamental principle of financial planning is the formation of a budget. A budget serves as a roadmap for entrepreneurs, outlining the projected income and expense over a specific point of clock. By creating and adhering to a budget, entrepreneurs can monitor their cash flowing and identify areas where saving can be made or investment can be increased. Additionally, budgeting allow entrepreneurs to have a clear understanding of their financial capability, enabling them to make informed decisions regarding the allotment of resource and the execution of growth strategies. Financial planning requires entrepreneurs to develop a comprehensive understanding of financial statements. Financial statements, such as the income statement, equilibrium shroud, and statement of cash flow, provide entrepreneurs with valuable insights into the financial wellness of their business. By analyzing these statements, entrepreneurs can identify trend, assess the profitability of their operation, and make strategic decisions to enhance business growth. For instance, a careful psychoanalysis of the income statement can provide entrepreneurs with insights into receipts source and price driver, allowing them to identify areas where receipts can be maximized or expense can be reduced. Financial planning necessitates entrepreneurs to think critically about their business financing options. Entrepreneurs must consider the various sources of uppercase available to them, such as fairness financing, debt financing, or crowdfunding. By understanding the advantage and disadvantage of each financing option, entrepreneurs can make informed decisions that align with their business goal and growth strategies. Additionally, financial planning requires entrepreneurs to consider the concept of risk management. Entrepreneurs must evaluate the potential risk associated with their business operation and develop strategies to mitigate or manage this risk. By implementing risk management strategies, entrepreneurs can safeguard their business against unforeseen event that may impact their financial constancy and growth prospect. Financial planning necessitates entrepreneurs to monitor and evaluate their financial performance on an ongoing fundament. By tracking key financial metric and performance indicator, entrepreneurs can assess the potency of their strategies and make necessary adjustment to drive business growth. For instance, by monitoring metric such as gross profits leeway, rejoin on investing, or cash changeover oscillation, entrepreneurs can identify areas where improvement can be made and take proactive measure to optimize their financial performance. The aim of this test is to provide entrepreneurs with a comprehensive understanding of financial principles and their application in business growth. By understanding financial planning, budgeting, financial statements, financing options, risk management, and financial performance valuation, entrepreneurs can effectively manage their money and make informed decisions that contribute to their business growth. The conception of budget is one that is essential for entrepreneurs to understand and implement in order to effectively manage their money and grow their business. Budgeting involves the careful allotment of resource to different areas of the business in order to achieve financial goals. Without a budget, entrepreneurs risk overspending or allocating resource inefficiently, which can lead to cash flow problem and impede business growth. By creating a budget, entrepreneurs can gain a clear understanding of their financial commitment and make informed decisions about where to allocate their resource. A budget provides a roadmap for financial achiever, allowing entrepreneurs to track receipts and expenses, set target, and make adjustment when necessary. This can help entrepreneurs identify areas where cost can be reduced, receipts can be increased, and resource can be reallocated to support business growth. Additionally, a budget enables entrepreneurs to monitor their cash flow, which is crucial for sustaining operation on a day-to-day fundament. By understanding the timing and amount of cash coming into the business, as well as the timing and amount of cash going out, entrepreneurs can make better decisions about managing their working uppercase. This can include ensuring that invoice are sent out promptly and collecting payment from customer in a timely way, as well as manage expenses to avoid unnecessary cash outflows. By effectively managing cash flow, entrepreneurs can minimize the danger of running out of money and maximize their ability to invest in growth initiative. In plus to budget, entrepreneurs must also have a clear understanding of their business's financial statements in order to effectively manage their money and make informed financial decisions. Financial statements, such as the income statement, balance sheet, and cash flow statement, provide a snapshot of a business's financial performance, stance, and cash flows, respectively. By analyzing these statements, entrepreneurs can gain insights into the financial wellness of their business and identify areas for improvement. The income statement shows the receipts generated and expenses incurred over a specific point of time, allowing entrepreneurs to evaluate profitability and identify opportunity to increase receipts or reduce cost. The balance sheet provides a snapshot of a business's asset, liability, and fairness at a particular level in time, helping entrepreneurs understand their business's liquid and financial stance. The cash flow statement shows the cash generated and used by the business during a specific point, providing entrepreneurs with valuable insights into the timing and generator of cash inflow and outflows. By understanding their financial statements, entrepreneurs can make informed decisions about price, expenses, investment, and funding, among other financial aspects of their business. Entrepreneurs must have a solid understanding of financial analysis technique in order to evaluate their business's financial performance and make informed decisions about its next. Financial analysis involves the interpreting of financial information to assess a business's performance, profitability, liquid, solvency, and efficiency, among other aspects. By analyzing financial ratios, trend, and benchmark, entrepreneurs can identify strengths, weaknesses, opportunity, and threat related to their business's financial performance. Analyzing profitability ratios can help entrepreneurs evaluate their business's ability to generate profit, while analyzing liquid ratios can help entrepreneurs assess their business's ability to meet short-term obligation. By conducting financial analysis, entrepreneurs can identify areas for improvement, develop strategy to address weaknesses, and capitalize on strengths, all of which are crucial for growing a successful business. Understanding fundamental financial principles and how to apply them is essential for entrepreneurs looking to effectively manage their money and grow their business. By implementing budget practice, analyzing financial statements, and conducting financial analysis, entrepreneurs can make informed financial decisions that support business growth and sustainability. While these financial principles can seem complex and intimidate, there are many resources available to help entrepreneurs develop their financial literacy and skill. With the correct cognition and tool, entrepreneurs can navigate the financial aspects of their business with trust and achieve their financial goals.

II. UNDERSTANDING FINANCIAL STATEMENTS

Understanding financial statements is important for entrepreneurs as it provides them with valuable insights into the financial health and performance of their business. One of the key financial statements that entrepreneurs need to understand is the income statement, also known as the profit and departure statement. The income statement provides a succinct of a company's revenue, expense, and net income for a specific period. By analyzing the income statement, entrepreneurs can determine their company's profitability and identify areas of betterment. They can identify which products or service are generating the most receipts and focus their resource on those areas. Additionally, the income statement can help entrepreneurs assess their company's financial performance over time by comparing income statements from different period. This allows them to gauge whether their business is growing or declining and make informed decisions accordingly. Another important financial statement that entrepreneurs need to be familiar with is the balance sheet. The balance sheet provides a snap of a company's financial stance at a specific level in time and consist of three component : asset, liability, and owner's fairness. Asset include tangible and intangible item such as cash, inventorying, and belongings. Indebtedness represent a company's obligations, such as loan and account payable. Owner's fairness reflects the owner's investing in the business and any retained profits. By reviewing the balance sheet, entrepreneurs can evaluate their company's financial constancy, liquidity, and leveraging. They can assess whether their asset is sufficient to cover their liability and determine the ratio of debt financing in their uppercase construction. This information is crucial for making financial decisions, such as obtaining additional financing or managing cash flow more effectively. In plus to the income statement and balance sheet, entrepreneurs should also understand the statement of cash flows. The statement of cash flows provides information about a company's cash inflow and outflow during a specific period. This statement is divided into three section : operational activities, investing activities, and financing activities. By analyzing the statement of cash flows, entrepreneurs can gain insights into the company's source and use of cash. They can determine whether the company is generating sufficient cash from its day-to-day operation, investing in increase opportunity, and financing its activities. This information is crucial for managing cash flow, which is essential for the endurance and increase of any business. By regularly monitoring the statement of cash flows, entrepreneurs can identify potential cash flow problem in advanced and take necessary actions to address them. Entrepreneurs should also be familiar with financial ratios, which are derived from the information provided in the financial statements. Financial ratios are used to evaluate a company's financial performance, liquidity, solvency, and profitability. Some commonly used ratios include the current ratio, quick ratio, rejoin on fairness, and gross profit leeway. By calculating and analyzing these ratios, entrepreneurs can gain insights into their company's financial health and compare it to manufacture benchmark. A low liquidity ratio may indicate that the company has insufficient cash to meet its short-term obligations, while a high gross profit leeway may suggest that the company is pricing its products or service too high. By understanding and interpreting financial ratios, entrepreneurs can make informed decisions and take appropriate actions to improve their company's financial performance. Understanding financial statements is essential for entrepreneurs to effectively manage their money and grow their business. By analyzing the income statement, balance sheet, statement of cash flows, and financial ratios, entrepreneurs can gain valuable insights into their company's financial health, performance, and cash flow. This information is crucial for making informed decisions, identifying areas of betterment, and ensuring the long-term achiever of their business. Entrepreneurs should invest time and attempt in understanding and interpreting these financial statements.

FINANCIAL STATEMENTS: BALANCE SHEET, INCOME STATEMENT AND CASH FLOW STATEMENT

The cash flow statement is another financial statement that provides info about the cash inflows and outflows of a business during a specific point. It presents the change in cash and cash equivalent by categorizing them into operational activities, investing activities, and financing activities. Operate activities include the cash flows from primary business operations such as sale receipt, payment to supplier, and payroll expense. Investing activities involve cash flows related to the acquirement and disposition of long-term assets, including purchasing or selling belongings, flora, and equipment or making investment in other entity. Financing activities encompass cash flows from obtaining or repaying uppercase from owner or external source, such as issuance or purchasing back share, borrowing or repaying loan, or paying dividend. By examining the cash flow statement, entrepreneurs can assess the company's ability to generate cash from its operations, evaluate its investing decisions, and determine its dependency on external financing. It helps entrepreneurs in identifying the source and use of cash, which is essential for making effective financial decisions and managing liquid. Understanding financial statements is crucial for entrepreneurs to effectively manage their money and grow their business. The equilibrium shroud provides a snap of a company's financial stance at a specific level in clock, including its assets, liability, and proprietor's fairness. It aids entrepreneurs in calculating important ratio and making informed decisions about financing, investment, and overall execution. The income statement, on the other paw, depicts a company's financial execution over a specific point by summarizing its revenue, expense, and net income or departure. Entrepreneurs can use this statement to analyze the profitability and evaluate the potency of their business operations. The cash flow statement tracks the inflows and outflows of cash, enabling entrepreneurs to assess their company's ability to generate cash, handle liquid, and make effective financial decisions. By fully grasping these financial statements and their significance, entrepreneurs can gain valuable insight into their business's financial wellness, identify area for betterment, and make informed decisions that contribute to the increase and achiever of their venture.

ANALYZING FINANCIAL STATEMENTS FOR DECISION-MAKING

Analyzing financial statements is of utmost importance for decision-making in a business as it provides entrepreneurs with valuable insights into the financial wellness and execution of their company. By examining financial statements, such as the income statement, balance sheet, and cash flow statement, entrepreneurs can assess the profitability, liquidity, and solvency of their business, enabling them to make informed decisions that drive the growth and success of their venture. One key cause why analyzing financial statements is crucial for decision-making is the ability to evaluate profitability. The income statement, also known as the profit and departure statement, presents detailed information on a company's revenue, expense, and net income. By examining this statement, entrepreneurs can gain valuable insights into the sources of their receipts and the cost associated with generating that receipts. This analysis allows entrepreneurs to identify the most profitable component of their business and allocate resource accordingly. For instance, if a particular merchandise or servicing contribute significantly to the overall receipts while incurring lower cost, entrepreneurs can focus on promote and developing that product/service further to increase profitability. On the other paw, if certain expense are excessively high, entrepreneurs can identify area where cost-cutting measure can be implemented to improve the overall profitability of the business. Financial statements provide entrepreneurs with insights into their business's liquidity, which is the ability to meet short-term obligations. This information is particularly important for decision-making as it enables entrepreneurs to anticipate and manage cash flow challenges effectively. The balance sheet, for instance, provides a snap of a company's asset, liability, and fairness at a specific level in clock. By analyzing this statement, entrepreneurs can determine the liquidity of their business by comparing current asset (such as cash and account receivable) to current liability (such as account payable and short-term debt) . This analysis allows entrepreneurs to ensure that they have sufficient cash and other liquid asset to cover their short-term obligations, such as paying supplier or employee. By closely monitoring liquidity through the analysis of financial statements, entrepreneurs can make more informed decisions about managing cash flow and seek necessary financing options if needed. In plus to profitability and liquidity, financial statements also provide insights into a business's solvency, which is the ability to meet long-term obligations. The cash flow statement, in particular, showcases the sources and use of cash during a specific point, providing information on a company's ability to generate positive cash flows from its operation. By analyzing this statement, entrepreneurs can assess whether their business generate enough cash to meet its long-term debt obligations, such as lend repayment or rent payment. This analysis is essential for decision-making as it helps entrepreneurs evaluate their business's financial stability and make proactive decisions to ensure solvency. For instance, if a business is consistently generating negative cash flows from its operation, entrepreneurs can identify strategy to improve operational efficiency or seek additional financing options to cover long-term obligations. Analyzing financial statements is of great importance for decision-making as it allows entrepreneurs to evaluate the profitability, liquidity, and solvency of their business. By examining financial statements, entrepreneurs can identify the most profitable aspect of their business, manage cash flow effectively, and ensure the long-term financial stability of their venture. Armed with this cognition, entrepreneurs can make informed decisions that drive the growth and success of their business, while also mitigating potential risk and challenge. It is essential for entrepreneurs to understand and analyze financial statements to achieve their business objective.

TECHNIQUES FOR INTERPRETING FINANCIAL STATEMENTS ACCURATELY

Another important proficiency for interpreting financial statements accurately is to understand the conception of profitability ratios. Profitability ratios are used to measure the company's ability to generate profit from its operations. One common profitability ratio is the gross profit margin, which is calculated by dividing the gross profit by the net sales. The gross profit margin provides an indication of how efficiently the company is manufacturing or purchasing its products. A high gross profit margin means that the company is able to command a high cost for its products and/or has a low price of commodity sold. Another important profitability ratio is the net profit margin, which is calculated by dividing the net income by the net sales. The net profit margin shows how much profit the company is able to generate from its sales after all expense are taken into calculate. It is important to compare these profitability ratios with manufacture average to get a better understanding of how the company is performing relative to its competitor. In plus to profitability ratios, liquidity ratios are also crucial in interpreting financial statements accurately. Liquidity ratios measure the company's ability to meet its short-term obligations. One such ratio is the current ratio, which is calculated by dividing the current assets by the current liabilities. The current ratio provides an indication of the company's ability to pay off its short-term debt using its short-term assets. A high current ratio indicates that the company is in a strong financial position and is able to meet its current obligations without trouble. Another liquidity ratio is the quick ratio, which is calculated by subtracting inventorying from current assets and dividing the consequence of current liabilities. The quick ratio provides a more conservative measure of the company's liquidity as it excludes inventorying, which may not be easily converted into cash. When interpreting liquidity ratios, it is important to consider the nature of the business and its specific working uppercase requirement. Cash flow statements are another instrument for interpreting financial statements accurately. Cash flow statements provide info on the cash inflow and outflow of a company during a specific point. They include three sections : operating activities, investing activities, and financing activities. The operating activities segment shows the cash generated or used in the company's nucleus business operations. The investing activities segment reflects cash flows related to acquisition or sales of long-term assets. The financing activities segment includes cash flows from issuing or repaying debt and fairness. By analyzing the cash flow statement, an entrepreneur can assess the company's ability to generate cash from its operations, its investing activities, and its financing decision. This is crucial in understanding the company's cash position and its ability to invest in increase opportunity or meet its financial obligations. Understanding technique for interpreting financial statements accurately is essential for entrepreneurs in managing their finances and growing their businesses. This technique include analyzing the income statement, equilibrium shroud, and cash flow statement, as well as calculating and comparing key financial ratios. By taking a comprehensive overture to analyzing financial statements, entrepreneurs can gain valuable insight into their company's financial wellness, profitability, liquidity, and cash flow. This cognition allows entrepreneurs to make informed financial decision, allocate resource effectively, and identify area for betterment. With a solid understanding of financial statements and the ability to interpret them accurately, entrepreneurs can take command of their finances and drive the achiever of their businesses. Effective financial management is essential for entrepreneurs to successfully grow their business. By understanding fundamental financial principle and applying them to their operation, entrepreneurs can make informed decision and increase their chance of success. It is important for entrepreneurs to create a detailed financial program, including projecting future cash flow and understanding their financial execution indicator. By doing so, entrepreneurs can identify potential risk and take appropriate measure to mitigate them. Additionally, entrepreneurs should track and monitor their financial activity regularly and make adjustment as necessary. They should also consider alternative source of funding and explore opportunity to maximize their profitability. Leveraging engineering and package can streamline financial process and provide entrepreneurs with real-time financial info. Financial management is a crucial facet of entrepreneurship, and by mastering this principle, entrepreneurs can set themselves up for long-term success.

III. BUDGETING AND FORECASTING

Budgeting involve planning and allocating financial resources to achieve specific business goals and objectives. It helps entrepreneurs to monitor and control their expenditure, identify potential area of betterment, and make informed decisions about resource allocation. By creating a budget, entrepreneurs can set realistic target and priority, allocate fund accordingly, and track their progression towards achieving their financial goals. It also allows entrepreneurs to identify potential risks and develop strategies to mitigate them. Forecasting, on the other paw, involves estimating future financial outcome based on historical information, market trends, and other relevant factors. It enables entrepreneurs to predict next revenues, expenses, and cash flow, which is crucial for making informed business decisions. By accurately forecasting their financials, entrepreneurs can anticipate potential challenge, identify opportunity for increase, and make necessary adjustment to their strategies. It also helps entrepreneurs to evaluate the financial feasibility of their business idea and determine whether they can achieve their desired outcome. In ordering to create an effective budget and forecast, entrepreneurs need to have a deep understand of their business operation, market dynamic, and financial performance. They must analyze and assess their historical financial information to identify trends, pattern, and key driver of financial performance. This psychoanalysis will provide important insight into the factors that regulate revenues, expenses, and profitability, enabling entrepreneurs to make more accurate forecasts and budgets.

Entrepreneurs should also consider external factors that can impact their business, such as change in the economic surroundings, manufacture regulation, and client preference. By keeping abreast of manufacture trends and market weather, entrepreneurs can make more accurate prediction about future requirement, competitor, and pricing. This will enable them to develop more effective strategies for resource allocation, merchandising, and pricing. In plus, entrepreneurs need to involve key stakeholders in the budgeting and forecasting procedure to ensure alignment and accountability. By seeking comment from employee, supplier, and customer, entrepreneurs can gain valuable insight and perspective that can help improve the truth and potency of their budgets and forecasts. It also fosters a feel of possession and obligation among stakeholders, enhancing their dedication to achieving the business's financial goals. Entrepreneurs must regularly monitor and evaluate their budgets and forecasts to ensure they remain relevant and effective. They should compare actual financial performance to the budgeted figure and analyze any variance. This will help them identify area where they have deviated from their plan and take corrective activity if necessary. By regularly reviewing their budgets and forecasts, entrepreneurs can stay on racetrack, make necessary adjustment, and ensure that their financial direction strategies are aligned with their business objectives. Effective budgeting and forecasting are critical for entrepreneurs to manage their finance and achieve their business goals. By creating realistic budgets based on accurate forecasts, entrepreneurs can allocate their financial resources more effectively, monitor their performance, and make informed decisions. Budgeting and forecasting also help entrepreneurs identify potential risks and opportunity, enabling them to develop strategies to mitigate risks and capitalize on opportunity. By involving key stakeholders in the procedure and regularly monitor and evaluating their budgets and forecasts, entrepreneurs can ensure alignment and accountability, enhancing their chance of achiever in the dynamic and competitive business surroundings.

BUDGETING IN FINANCIAL PLANNING

It helps them set clear financial goals and allocate resources effectively. By creating a budget, entrepreneurs can identify areas where they can cut cost or increase profitability. It also enables them to anticipate and plan for future financial challenges and expenses. A well-designed budget can serve as a roadmap for their business, guiding their decision-making procedure and ensuring that they stay on track towards their financial objectives. Additionally, budgeting allows entrepreneurs to monitor their financial performance, compare their actual results with their projection, and make necessary adjustments as needed. This helps them identify areas of improvement and make informed decisions to optimize their financial resources. Budgeting also promotes financial discipline and accountability, as entrepreneurs are aware of their spending patterns and can control unnecessary expenses. Budgeting provides entrepreneurs with a sense of financial control and empowerment. They gain a better understand of their business's financial health and can make strategic decisions accordingly. This is particularly important for entrepreneurs seeking financing or investors, as having a well-designed budget demonstrates their financial frightfulness and their ability to achieve their financial target. Budgeting is an essential instrument for entrepreneurs to effectively manage their finances and grow their business. One of the key reason why budgeting is important for financial planning is that it helps entrepreneurs set clear financial goals. By establishing specific financial objectives, entrepreneurs can determine how many receipts they need to generate and identify cost-saving measure to achieve those goals. A budget can help break down long-term goals into short-term achievable target, allowing entrepreneurs to better align their day-to-day operation with their financial objectives. This enables them to monitor their progression and make necessary adjustments if they are not on track to meeting their goals. Budgeting allows entrepreneurs to allocate resources effectively. By identifying the areas that require the most investing, entrepreneurs can ensure that they allocate their financial resources to the most critical aspect of their business. This helps them make efficient utilize of their fund and avoid overspending on areas that may not contribute significantly to their overall growth. Additionally, budgeting enables entrepreneurs to anticipate and plan for future financial challenges and expenses. By estimating their future cash flow, entrepreneurs can determine if they have sufficient fund to cover upcoming expenses or financial obligation. This allows them to plan ahead and make informed decisions, such as securing additional financing or adjusting their business strategy to mitigate potential financial risk. Budgeting allows entrepreneurs to monitor their financial performance and make necessary adjustments. By comparing their actual results with their projected financial information, entrepreneurs can evaluate their business's financial health and identify areas of improvement. This enables them to make informed decisions to optimize their financial resources and improve their profitability. For instance, if a certain section consistently exceeds its budget, entrepreneurs can investigate the underlying reason and take appropriate action, such as implementing cost-cutting measure or reallocating resources. Budgeting promotes financial discipline and accountability. Entrepreneurs become more aware of their spending patterns and can control unnecessary expenses. This can significantly improve their financial direction and lend to the overall growth and achiever of their business. In summary, budgeting is a critical facet of financial planning for entrepreneurs. It helps them set clear financial goals, allocate resources effectively, anticipate future financial challenges, and monitor their financial performance. By creating a budget, entrepreneurs can make informed decisions and optimize their financial resources to achieve their business objectives. Budgeting also promotes financial discipline and accountability, which is crucial for entrepreneurs seeking financing or investors. Budgeting provides entrepreneurs with a sense of financial control and empowerment, enabling them to effectively manage their finances and grow their business.

STEPS INVOLVED IN CREATING A BUDGET FOR A BUSINESS

One important step involved in creating a budget for a business is identifying and estimating the revenue sources. This involves understanding the different revenue stream that the business generate and forecasting the potential income from each source. For instance, a retail business may generate revenue from sale of product, while a service-based business may generate revenue from customer fee. By analyzing historical information and market trend, entrepreneurs can estimate the potential revenue from each source. It is important to be realistic and conservative in these estimate to avoid overestimating the revenue and ending up with a budget that is not feasible. Another crucial step is analyzing and estimating the fixed and variable expenses. Fixed expenses refer to costs that remain constant irrespective of the business's level of activity, such as lease or rent payment, indemnity premium, and salary. Variable expenses, on the other paw, vacillate based on the level of business activity, such as raw material, direct toil costs, and marketing expenses. It is necessary to carefully assess the fixed and variable expenses to understand their effect on the overall budget. By accurately estimating these expenses, entrepreneurs can determine the sum of revenue required to cover them and ensure that the budget is realistic and achievable. Additionally, creating a budget involves setting financial goals for the business. This step is important as it provides a feel of way and aim for financial plan. Financial goals can vary depending on the nature of the business, but common objective may include increasing profitability, achieving a specific sale objective, reducing costs, or improving cash flowing. By setting clear and measurable financial goals, entrepreneurs can align their budget effort with their overall business objective and ensure that the financial plan is aligned with the long-term sight of the business. Once the revenue sources, expenses, and financial goals have been estimated, the next step is to allocate funds accordingly. This involves breaking down the budget into different category and assigning specific amount to each. Category may include sale and marketing expenses, operational costs, inquiry and developing, and administrative expenses. It is important to allocate funds based on the precedence and grandness of each class and to ensure that all necessary expenses are adequately covered. This step requires careful circumstance and examination to avoid overspending and to optimize resourcefulness allotment. Another important step is monitoring and reviewing the budget regularly. A budget is not a static paper and should be treated as a dynamic instrument that requires constant monitoring and readjustment. By regularly reviewing the budget, entrepreneurs can assess whether it is on racetrack, identify any deviation, and take corrective action if necessary. Monitoring the budget allows entrepreneurs to compare the actual execution with the budgeted amount, identify any variance, and understand the reason behind them. This enables them to make informed decisions and adjustment to the budget, ensuring that it remains realistic and aligned with the changing business surroundings. In summary, creating a budget for a business involves several important steps. These step include identifying and estimating revenue sources, analyzing and estimating expenses, setting financial goals, allocating funds, and monitoring and reviewing the budget regularly. By following these step, entrepreneurs can develop a comprehensive and realistic financial plan that can serve as a roadmap for managing their money and growing their business. A well-designed budget is a valuable instrument for entrepreneurs, helping them make informed decisions and achieve their financial objective.

TECHNIQUES FOR ACCURATE FORECASTING TO ANTICIPATE FUTURE FINANCIAL NEEDS

One such technique is the use of historical financial data and trend analysis. By analyzing past financial statement and comparing them with industry trends, entrepreneurs can identify pattern and trends that can help in predicting future financial needs. If a business experienced a consistent increase in receipts over the past few days, it is likely that this increase trend will continue in the future, and the entrepreneur can plan for enlargement or increased investing accordingly. Similarly, if a business has been consistently experiencing cash flowing issue during a particular point each year, the entrepreneur can anticipate this and make necessary arrangement to ensure sufficient fund to cover expense during that clock. Another technique for accurate forecasting is the use of financial models and simulations. Financial models are mathematical representation of a business's operation, which can be used to project future financial performance under different scenario. By inputting various assumptions, such as receipts increase rate, price structure, and market weather, entrepreneurs can simulate different outcome and identify potential risks and opportunity. This enables entrepreneurs to make more informed decisions and anticipate future financial needs. If a business is considering introducing a new merchandise pipeline, a financial model can help assess the potential financial affect and guide the entrepreneur in making appropriate investing decisions. Entrepreneurs can also use benchmarking as a technique for accurate forecasting. Benchmarking involve comparing a business's financial performance to that of its competitors or industry peer. By analyzing key financial ratio, such as profitability, liquid, and efficiency, entrepreneurs can identify area of potency and helplessness in their business and gain insights into how it is positioned against its competitors. This information can be invaluable in predicting future financial needs. For instance, if a business's profits leeway is significantly lower than that of its competitors, it may indicate inefficiency or pricing issue that need to be addressed. By making improvement in this area, the entrepreneur can anticipate increased profitability and plan for future financial needs accordingly. In plus to the aforementioned technique, entrepreneurs can also utilize market research and customer feedback as tool for accurate forecasting. Market research involves gathering and analyzing data about the target market, industry trends, and customer preferences. By understanding the needs and preferences of their target market, entrepreneurs can better forecast future requirement and adjust their financial plans accordingly. For instance, if market research indicates a shifting in customer preferences towards eco-friendly product, an entrepreneur can anticipate increased requirement for such product and invest in research and developing to meet that requirement. Similarly, customer feedback plays a vital role in accurate forecasting. By soliciting feedback from existing customer, entrepreneurs can gain insights into their gratification level with existing product or service, as well as identify potential area for betterment. This information can help in forecasting future sale and receipts, as satisfied customer are more likely to continue purchasing from the business. By addressing customer concern and improving the overall customer feel, entrepreneurs can build customer allegiance and generate repetition business, which can significantly impact future financial needs. Accurate forecasting technique are essential for entrepreneurs to anticipate future financial needs effectively. By utilizing historical data and trend analysis, financial models and simulations, benchmarking, market research, and customer feedback, entrepreneurs can make informed decisions, identify potential risks and opportunity, and adjust their financial plans accordingly. This technique provide entrepreneurs with the necessary tool to navigate the challenge of managing their finance and grow their business successfully. Entrepreneurs must also consider the concept of financial leverage when managing their money and growing their business. Financial leverage refer to utilize of borrowed funds or debt to finance a company's operations and investment. By utilizing financial leverage, entrepreneurs can potentially increase their returns on investing and accelerate the increase of their business. This scheme also comes with its own put of risk and consideration that entrepreneurs must carefully evaluate. One of the main advantage of financial leverage is the ability to amplify returns. By borrowing funds at a lower interest rate than the rate of return on the investing, entrepreneurs can generate additional profit. For instance, if an entrepreneur borrows $100,000 at a 4 % interest rate to invest in a design that yields a 6 % return, the entrepreneur would earn a 2 % return on the borrowed funds. This increased return can significantly enhance the profitability and increase possible of the business. Additionally, financial leverage allows entrepreneurs to conserve their own uppercase. Instead of using their own funds to finance their business operations and investment, entrepreneurs can utilize borrowed funds to free up their uppercase for other purpose. This can be particularly advantageous for entrepreneurs with limited personal resource or those who prefer to keep their personal finance separate from their business finance. It is important for entrepreneurs to exercise circumspection when using financial leverage. One of the main risks associated with financial leverage is the increased vulnerability to debt. Borrowing money comes with the duty to repay the debt, along with any associated interest or fee. If the business is unable to generate sufficient cash flow to repay the debt, it may face financial distress or even failure. Entrepreneurs must carefully assess their ability to generate consistent and predictable cash flow before employing financial leverage. It is crucial for entrepreneurs to understand the concept of leverage ratio when using financial leverage. The leverage ratio represents the ratio of debt in a company's uppercase construction. A higher leverage ratio indicates a higher grade of financial leverage, which can amplify returns but also increase the danger of financial distress. Entrepreneurs must strike an equilibrium between maximizing returns and maintaining a manageable tier of debt. Additionally, entrepreneurs must consider the cost of borrowing when utilizing financial leverage. Borrowing funds typically incurs interest cost, which can eat into the profitability of the business. Entrepreneurs must evaluate whether the potential returns on investing outweigh the cost of borrowing. This psychoanalysis should take into calculate not only the interest rate on the borrowed funds but also any associated fee or expense. Entrepreneurs should compare the cost of borrowing with alternative source of funding, such as fairness funding or self-funding, to determine the most cost-effective alternative for their business. Understanding and effectively applying financial principle is crucial for entrepreneurs when managing their money and growing their business. By developing a solid understand of concept such as cash flow direction, financial plan, and financial leverage, entrepreneurs can make informed decision and maximize the efficiency and profitability of their business operations. It is important for entrepreneurs to remain vigilant and regularly assess their financial stance to ensure the sustainability and long-term achiever of their venture. A sound financial groundwork can provide entrepreneurs with the trust and resource needed to navigate the ever-changing business landscape and achieve their entrepreneurial goal.

IV. MANAGING CASH FLOW

It refers to the procedure of monitor, analyzing, and optimizing the flow of cash into and out of a company. Efficient cash flow management is essential for sustaining daily operation, meeting financial obligation, and achieving long-term growth objectives. One of the primary challenges faced by many entrepreneurs is maintaining a positive cash flow. This requires careful plan and effective executing of strategy to ensure that the company has sufficient cash on paw to cover its expenses and invest in growth opportunity. The first stride in managing cash flow is to develop accurate cash flow projections. These forecast provide a detailed psychoanalysis of the expected cash inflow and outflow over a specific point, typically monthly or annually. By examining historical information and making reasonable assumption about future receipts and expenses, entrepreneurs can gain insight into their cash position and make informed decision. Cash flow projections allow business owner to identify potential cash shortfall and take prompt activity to address them. This could involve postponing non-essential expenditure, renegotiating payment terms with suppliers, or exploring additional financing options. To effectively manage cash flow, entrepreneurs must closely monitor their receivables and payables. Receivables refer to the money owed to the company by its customer, while payables represent the company's outstanding obligation to suppliers, lender, and other stakeholder. Slow-paying customer or an excessive amount of overdue invoice can severely impact cash flow. Entrepreneurs should establish clear recognition terms and procedure for invoice, ensure prompt follow-up on overdue payment, and consider implementing incentive or penalty to encourage timely payment. On the other paw, it is equally important to negotiate favorable payment terms with suppliers, such as extended recognition period or discount for early payment. By carefully managing receivables and payables, entrepreneurs can improve their cash flow position and reduce the danger of liquid problem. Another essential element of cash flow management is efficient inventory command. Inventory represents the commodity and material that a company holds for sale or output. Maintaining excessive inventory levels can tie up a significant amount of cash and increase holding costs. Conversely, running out of inventory can result in lost sale and damage the company's repute. Entrepreneurs must strike an equilibrium between having sufficient inventory to meet client requirement and minimizing carry costs. This requires implementing effective inventory management system, such as just-in-time (JIT) or economic ordering amount (ESQ) model. By accurately forecasting requirement, monitoring reorder point, and optimizing ordering quantity, entrepreneurs can ensure that their inventory levels align with their cash flow objectives. Entrepreneurs should consider establishing a cash reserve or eventuality stock to buffer against unforeseen event. These reserve can help cover unexpected expenses, emergency, or period of low cash flow. Setting aside a component of profit on a regular fundament can provide a financial safe earnings and reduce trust on external financing source. The amount of the cash reserve will depend on the company's specific circumstance, such as its manufacture, sizing, and danger visibility. In plus to maintaining a cash reserve, entrepreneurs should also explore other working uppercase financing options, such as line of recognition or deal recognition, to bridge temporary cash flow gap. Managing cash flow is a critical aspect of running a successful business. By developing accurate cash flow projections, closely monitoring receivables and payables, efficiently managing inventory, and establishing a cash reserve, entrepreneurs can ensure the smooth procedure of their businesses and achieve long-term growth objectives. While cash flow challenge are common among entrepreneurs, effective cash flow management strategy can help mitigate the risk and position the company for sustainable success. Through diligent financial plan, psychoanalysis, and executing, entrepreneurs can navigate the complexity of cash flow management and drive their businesses towards profitability and successfulness.

DEFINITION AND SIGNIFICANCE OF CASH FLOW MANAGEMENT

Essentially, it involves keeping racetrack of the inflows and outflows of cash to ensure that the business has enough liquidity to meet its short-term obligations. Cash flow management is of utmost significance for entrepreneurs as it directly impacts the survival, growth, and profitability of their businesses. One of the primary reason why cash flow management is crucial for entrepreneurs is its role in ensuring the survival of the business. Cash flow is the lifeblood of any business, as it allows entrepreneurs to pay for essential expense such as lease, salary, utility, and supplier invoice. Without proper cash flow management, a business can quickly run into financial difficulty, unable to meet its obligations and potentially facing failure. By closely monitoring the inflows and outflows of cash, entrepreneurs can identify potential cash shortage well in advanced and take necessary step to address them, such as securing additional funding or renegotiating payment terms with suppliers. Consequently, effective cash flow management helps entrepreneurs maintain the financial health and constancy of their businesses. Cash flow management is crucial for the growth and enlargement of a business. One of the main challenges faced by entrepreneurs is managing the time of cash inflows and outflows. For instance, a business may experience delay in receiving payment from customers, resulting in a temporary cash dearth. On the other paw, the business may have to make upfront payment to suppliers or invest in merchandising and ad campaign to attract new customers. In such situation, effective cash flow management becomes essential to ensure that the business has sufficient liquidity to cover its expense and seize growth opportunities. By accurately forecasting cash flows and executing robust cash flow management strategy, entrepreneurs can address these challenge proactively and capitalize on growth prospect. Cash flow management plays a vital role in enhancing the profitability of a business. By closely monitoring and effectively managing cash flows, entrepreneurs can identify area of potential betterment and enforce strategy to optimize cash utilization. For instance, they can negotiate payment terms with suppliers to allow for more extended payment cycle, freeing up cash for other purpose. They can also take vantage of discount for early payment or majority purchase, reducing cost and improving cash flow. Additionally, efficient cash flow management enables entrepreneurs to identify and address inefficiency in the collecting of receivables, such as implementing strict recognition policy, conducting creditworthiness check, and establishing clear payment terms with customers. By optimizing the time and utilization of cash, entrepreneurs can improve profitability and maximize return on their investment. Cash flow management is a critical aspect of financial management for entrepreneurs. It entails monitoring and managing the flow of cash into and out of a business, ensuring that it has sufficient liquidity to meet short-term obligations. Cash flow management is of utmost significance for entrepreneurs as it directly impacts the survival, growth, and profitability of their businesses. It helps ensure the survival of the business by enabling entrepreneurs to address potential cash shortage proactively. Effective cash flow man-

agement also facilitates business growth by allowing entrepreneurs to navigate time challenge and seize growth opportunities.
Additionally, it enhances profitability by optimizing cash utilization and identifying area for betterment. Entrepreneurs must prioritize cash flow management to ensure the financial health and
achiever of their businesses.

STRATEGIES FOR IMPROVING CASH FLOW EFFICIENCY

In ordering to improve cash flow efficiency, entrepreneurs can employ various strategy. One such strategy is to negotiate favorable payment terms with supplier. By negotiating extended payment terms, entrepreneurs can delay their cash outflows, allowing for more clock to generate receipts before needing to make payments. Additionally, entrepreneurs should consider implementing strict cash direction practice, such as monitoring cash inflows and outflows on a regular fundament. By closely monitoring cash flows, entrepreneurs can identify area where cash is being tied up unnecessarily and take step to rectify the position. Another strategy that can help improve cash flow efficiency is to encourage customer to make timely payments. This can be achieved by offering incentive for early payments or implementing late payment penalty. Entrepreneurs should analyze their inventory levels and objective to optimize them. By reducing excess inventory and ensure that the right sum of inventory is on paw, entrepreneurs can improve cash flow by minimizing tied-up uppercase. Entrepreneurs should review their accounts receivable to identify any overdue payments and take appropriate action to expedite their collecting. This may involve implementing stricter recognition policy or contacting customer directly to remind them of their outstanding invoice. Entrepreneurs should consider exploring alternative financing options to improve cash flow efficiency. This could include obtaining a pipeline of recognition or securing a LED to cover short-term cash need. By having admittance to additional uppercase, entrepreneurs can ensure that they can meet their financial obligation without straining cash flow. Another strategy for improving cash flow efficiency is to minimize overhead costs. This could involve renegotiating lease agreement, finding more cost-effective supplier, or implementing cost-cutting measure within the establishment. By reducing unnecessary expense, entrepreneurs can free up cash that can be used to fund the growth of the business or address any cash flow gap. Additionally, entrepreneurs should consider implementing cash flow forecasting. By projecting future cash inflows and outflows, entrepreneurs can anticipate potential cash flow challenge and take proactive measure to manage them. This could involve adjusting expenditure pattern, securing additional financing, or seeking opportunity to increase receipts. Entrepreneurs should consider establishing a cash reserve. By setting aside a component of their profit as a cash reserve, entrepreneurs can ensure that they have a safe earning in the issue of unexpected expense or economic downturn. This will provide pacification of psyche and reduce the financial stress on the business. Improving cash flow efficiency is crucial for the achiever and sustainability of any business. By implementing strategy such as negotiating payment terms, monitoring cash flows, encouraging timely client payments, optimizing inventory levels, reviewing accounts receivable, exploring alternative financing options, minimizing overhead costs, implementing cash flow forecasting, and establishing a cash reserve, entrepreneurs can effectively manage their cash flows and ensure the long-term growth of their business. This strategy require careful plan and regular monitoring, but the benefit of improved cash flow efficiency are well worth the attempt.

MONITORING AND ANALYZING CASH FLOW REGULARLY

The grandness of monitoring and analyzing cash flow regularly cannot be overstated for entrepreneurs. Cash flow is the lifeblood of any business, as it represents the drift of money in and out of the party. Monitoring cash flow allows entrepreneurs to have a real-time understanding of their business's financial health, enabling them to make informed decisions and take appropriate action to ensure the long-term success of their adventure. Regularly monitoring cash flow provides entrepreneurs with a clear photograph of how much money is coming into the business and how much is going out. By analyzing this info, entrepreneurs can identify any discrepancy or issue that may be affecting their cash flow. They may discover that their customer are not paying their invoice on clock, leading to a dearth of cash. This insight allows entrepreneurs to implement strategy to improve collection or renegotiate payment term, ensuring a steady flow of cash into the business. Monitoring cash flow enables entrepreneurs to identify pattern or trend in their business's financial execution. They can observe how cash flow fluctuates throughout the year, allowing them to anticipate period of high or low cash flow and program accordingly. This is particularly important for seasonal business, as they need to manage their cash flow during off-peak period when revenue are lower. By understanding these pattern, entrepreneurs can make strategic business decisions, such as adjusting inventorying level, staff, and merchandising effort, to align with expected change in cash flow. In plus to providing insight into day-to-day operations, monitoring cash flow also helps entrepreneurs evaluate the financial viability of their business over the long term. By regularly analyzing cash flow, entrepreneurs can determine whether their business is generating enough cash to cover its expense and meet its financial obligation. This is critical for making important business decisions, such as expanding operations, investing in new equipment, or seeking outside funding. By examining their cash flow, entrepreneurs can assess whether they have sufficient cash reserve to support their increase plan or if they need to secure additional financing to avoid cash shortage. Monitoring and analyzing cash flow regularly allows entrepreneurs to evaluate the potency of their financial strategy and make adjustment if necessary. They can assess the effect of offering discount or recognition term to customer on their cash flow and profitability. By reviewing cash flow report, entrepreneurs can identify area of inefficiency or wastefulness and implement cost-saving measure to improve their bottom pipeline. Another critical aspect of monitoring cash flow regularly is its part in managing risk and ensuring the financial constancy of the business. By identifying potential cash flow issue early on, entrepreneurs can take proactive step to mitigate risk and safeguard their business from financial unbalance. This may include building a cash stockpile to buffer against unexpected expense or economic downturn, establishing recognition line with financial institution, or diversifying receipts stream to reduce trust on a single client or marketplace. Monitoring and analyzing cash flow regularly is essential for entrepreneurs to understand the financial health of their business and make informed decisions. By closely monitoring cash flow, entrepreneurs can identify issue, anticipate trend, evaluate financial viability, adjust strategy, and handle risk effectively. Cash flow is a critical metric that must be managed diligently, as it impacts every aspect of a business's operations and long-term success. Entrepreneurs should prioritize monitoring and analyzing cash flow regularly to ensure the financial constancy and increase of their venture. Understanding and effectively managing finance is crucial for entrepreneurs to grow their business successfully. By familiarizing themselves with fundamental financial principles and implementing sound financial strategies, entrepreneurs can make informed decisions, downplay risk, and maximize profit. A solid understand of cash flowing, budgeting, financial statements, and evaluation allows entrepreneurs to track and allocate resource effectively, leading to better business outcomes. Entrepreneurs must also be aware of the different sources of finance available to them and the associated costs and risks. By diversifying their sources of financing, entrepreneurs can safeguard against financial instability and take vantage of opportunities for growth. Additionally, entrepreneurs should establish a financial plan and regularly monitor their business performance against their financial goal. This enables them to make adjustment as necessary and make informed decisions to optimize their business growth. Entrepreneurs should seek professional advice from financial expert and accountant who can provide direction and supporting in interpreting financial information and making strategic financial decisions. Entrepreneurs must also cultivate good financial habit such as maintaining accurate financial record, separating personal and business finance, and practicing prudent expenditure. By adhering to these financial principles, entrepreneurs can establish a solid groundwork for growth and navigate the financial challenge that may arise along their entrepreneurial journeying. In gist, finance is not just about number ; it is a fundamental aspect of entrepreneurship that underpins the success and sustainability of a business. In summary, finance plays a critical part in the success of entrepreneurs and their business. It provides the necessary model for decision-making, resourcefulness allotment, and growth. By understanding key financial principles and implementing effective financial strategies, entrepreneurs can navigate the complex financial landscape and optimize their business outcomes. Cash flowing direction, budgeting, financial statements, and evaluation are essential tool that entrepreneurs must master to ensure the efficient allotment of resource. Entrepreneurs must also consider the various sources of finance available to them and the associated costs and risks. By diversifying their financing and seeking professional advice, entrepreneurs can safeguard against financial instability and capitalize on opportunities for growth. Additionally, a well-defined financial plan and regular monitor of business performance assist entrepreneurs stay on track and make informed decisions. Cultivating good financial habit contribute to the overall financial wellness of the business and foster long-term success. Finance is a fundamental aspect of entrepreneurship that entrepreneurs must embrace to effectively manage their money and grow their business.

V. FINANCING OPTIONS FOR ENTREPRENEURS

Often face the daunting chore of finding the necessary fund to start or grow their business. Fortunately, there are various financing options available for entrepreneurs, each with its own advantages and disadvantage. One option is bootstrapping, which involves using personal saving or relying on friend and kinfolk for financial supporting. Bootstrapping allow for maximum command and tractability as entrepreneurs are not beholden to outside investor. It may limit the increase possible of the business due to a deficiency of sufficient capital. Another option is crowdfunding, which has gained popularity in recent days. Crowdfunding involves raising fund from a large amount of individual through online platform. This method not only provides access to capital but also serves as a merchandising instrument, allowing entrepreneurs to gain vulnerability and test the marketplace for their merchandise or servicing. Entrepreneurs need to actively promote their crusade and may face challenge in standing out among the throng of other project seeking funding. A more traditional financing option is seeking funding from bank or financial institution. This involves applying for loan or line of recognition, which can provide entrepreneurs with the necessary capital to start or expand their business. Bank often require a solid business program, confirmation, and a good recognition chronicle to grant funding. While this method provides access to significant fund, it also carries the danger of debt and concern payment. Additionally, bank may not be willing to lend to startups without a proven racetrack disc. Another option is venture capital financing, which involves seeking investing from venture capitalists. This investor provide funding in interchange for fairness in the party and often have manufacture expertness and connection that can benefit the entrepreneurs. While venture capital can inject a significant sum of capital into the business and provide valuable supporting, entrepreneurs may have to give up a component of their possession and decision-making force. Venture capitalists typically invest in high-growth potential business, making it a more suitable option for certain industry. Entrepreneurs can explore government grants and subsidy. Government often provides supporting to entrepreneurs through grants, taxation incentive, or subsidy for specific industry or activity. These program vary depending on the nation and can significantly alleviate the financial onus of starting or growing a business. Government grants may be subject to strict eligibility criterion and extensive coating processes, making them a more time-consuming funding option. Entrepreneurs need to carefully consider their specific business need, increase prospect, and danger permissiveness when choosing a financing option. It is crucial for entrepreneurs to have a solid understand of their financial position, including their current cash flowing, projected receipts, and expense, as well as their long-term financial goal. This cognition will enable entrepreneurs to assess which financing options align best with their business objective. Additionally, entrepreneurs should approach multiple source of funding and consider a combining of financing options, as relying on a single generator may limit their options or create dependence. By diversifying their financing source, entrepreneurs can mitigate financial risk and increase their likeliness of securing fund. Financing is a critical facet of entrepreneurship, as it provides the necessary capital to start or grow a business. With an array of financing options available, entrepreneurs can select the method that best suit their need and preference. Whether it be bootstrapping, crowdfunding, deposit loan, venture capital, or government grants, each option has its advantages and disadvantage, and entrepreneurs should carefully evaluate their choice. By understanding the financial principle and strategy underlying these financing options, entrepreneurs can manage their money effectively, minimize risk, and stance their business for long-term increase and achiever.

DIFFERENT FINANCING OPTIONS AVAILABLE TO ENTREPRENEURS: EQUITY FINANCING, DEBT FINANCING, CROWDFUNDING, ETC.

One of the most critical aspect of starting and growing a successful business is understanding the different financing options available to entrepreneurs. Financing is the lifeblood of any initiative, and choosing the right method can make a globe of divergence in achieving long-term success. There are several options that entrepreneurs can explore to fund their venture, such as equity financing, debt financing, and crowdfunding. Equity financing is a method of obtaining capital by selling share of possession in the party to investor. This type of financing is often seen in the early stage of a business, especially when the entrepreneur lacks personal fund to invest. In exchange for the financial supporting, investor receive a percent of the party's possession. Equity financing can come from various sources, including angel investor, adventure capitalist, and even friend and kinfolk member. While equity financing can provide a significant sum of capital to entrepreneurs, it also means giving up a component of command and potential next profit. Entrepreneurs need to carefully consider the advantages and disadvantage of equity financing before making a determination, as it can have a profound impact on the future way of the business. Debt financing, on the other hand, involves borrowing money from various source with the hope of refund with concern. This method of financing is widely used by entrepreneurs as it allows them to maintain command over their party while still accessing the necessary fund. Debt financing options include traditional deposit loan, line of recognition, and government-backed loan. Entrepreneurs must assess their creditworthiness and come up with a convince business program to secure these loan successfully. While debt financing can provide immediate fund, it also creates a financial indebtedness that needs to be repaid regardless of the business's success or loser. Entrepreneurs need to be mindful of their power to make repayment and manage their cash flowing effectively to avoid the pitfall of excessive debt. In recent days, crowdfunding has emerged as an alternative financing option for entrepreneurs. Crowdfunding involve raising fund from a large amount of individual, usually through online platform. Entrepreneurs present their business idea or prototype to potential investor or supporter who can contribute fund in exchange for a payoff or a stake in the party. Crowdfunding provides a unique chance for entrepreneurs to not only secure capital but also validate their business idea and build a community of loyal customer. It requires a well-crafted crusade and a compelling tale to attract enough concern and funding. Additionally, entrepreneurs need to carefully manage their relationship with crowdfunding backer to ensure transparency and answerability throughout the procedure. In plus to these traditional financing method, entrepreneurs can also consider alternative options such as grants and bootstrapping. Grants are non-repayable fund provided by administration agency, foundation, or organization to support specific project or initiative. Entrepreneurs need to identify eligible grants and prepare convincing application to secure this type of funding. Bootstrapping, on the other hand, involves using personal saving or reinvesting profit within the business to fund its increase. This method requires entrepreneurs to be frugal and resourceful, as it often means forgoing immediate reward in prefer of long-term success. Understanding the different financing options available to entrepreneurs is crucial for their business's success. Equity financing, debt financing, crowdfunding, grants, and bootstrapping are all viable method of obtaining capital, each with its advantages and challenge. Entrepreneurs need to carefully evaluate their business's need and goal to select the most appropriate financing option. They must also consider factor such as command, refund term, and the impact on future profitability. By making informed decision about financing, entrepreneurs can set themselves up for sustainable increase and successfulness in their business endeavor.

PROS AND CONS OF EACH FINANCING OPTION

One of the most common financing options is debt financing, which involves borrowing money from a loaner and paying it back with interest over a point of time. The advantage of debt financing is that it allows entrepreneurs to maintain full ownership and control of their business while accessing the uppercase they need to grow. Additionally, the interest paid on these loans may be taxation deductible, providing some financial succor. There are some drawback to debt financing as well. For one, it can be difficult for entrepreneurs with limited recognition chronicle or poor recognition score to secure loans. Taking on too much debt can lead to a heavy financial burden, especially if the business experiences a downswing or struggle to generate sufficient cash flowing to meet its loan obligation. Another financing option available to entrepreneurs is equity financing, which involves selling a portion of the business in interchange for uppercase. This can be done through private investors, adventure capitalist, or even going public and selling share on the inventory market. The advantage of equity financing is that it does not require entrepreneurs to take on debt or make regular loan payment. Instead, investors become partial owners of the business and deal in its future profit. This can be particularly beneficial for entrepreneurs with limited personal fund or a deficiency of confirmation to secure loans. Additionally, bringing in equity investors can provide valuable expertise, mentorship, and networking opportunity. There are some downsides to equity financing as well. For one, entrepreneurs must be willing to give up a portion of their ownership and control of the business. This means that they may have to consult with and receive approving from investors on important business decision. Investors may have higher expectation for return on their investing, putting increased squeeze on the entrepreneur to deliver strong financial execution. A less traditional financing option available to entrepreneurs is crowdfunding. With the rising of the cyberspace and social medium, crowdfunding has become an increasingly popular path for individual to raise fund for their business venture. This involves soliciting small amount of money from a large amount of masses through online platform. The advantage of crowdfunding is that it can provide entrepreneurs with admittance to a broad pond of potential investors, including individual who may not typically invest in business. Additionally, crowdfunding allows entrepreneurs to gauge market interest and receive feedback on their merchandise or servicing before fully launching. There are some challenge with crowdfunding as well. Contest for funding can be fierce, and entrepreneurs must have a comped and unique valuate proposal to stand out among the crowd. Additionally, crowdfunding campaign require significant time and effort to plan, execute, and handle, which can divert care and resource away from other business activity. There are various financing options available to entrepreneurs, each with its own put of advantage and disadvantage. Debt financing allows entrepreneurs while maintaining control of their business, but it can be difficult to obtain and may lead to a heavy financial burden. Equity financing provides entrepreneurs with uppercase and valuable expertise, but it requires them to give up ownership and control of their business. Crowdfunding offers a unique path to raise fund and exam market interest but requires significant time and effort. Entrepreneurs must carefully evaluate each financing option and choose the one that aligns with their business goal, financial capability, and danger permissiveness.

FACTORS TO CONSIDER WHEN CHOOSING THE MOST SUITABLE FINANCING OPTION FOR A BUSINESS

The first essential factor to take into calculate is the cost of financing. Entrepreneurs need to determine the total cost of borrow, including concern rate, fee, and charge, to assess the affordability and sustainability of the financing option. This will enable them to evaluate whether the potential benefit derived from the financing option outweigh its cost, and if it aligns with the business's financial goal. Another critical factor is the repayment terms and weather. Entrepreneurs need to carefully review the repayment docket, including the frequency and duration of payment, to ensure they can meet the financial obligation without jeopardizing the cash flowing and overall constancy of the business. Tractability in repayment options and the power to negotiate terms with the loaner can also be advantageous in managing business finance effectively. In plus to cost and repayment terms, entrepreneurs should also consider the tier of danger associated with different financing options. Debt financing, for instance, requires regular payment and poses a danger of nonpayment if the business experiences financial difficulty. Conversely, fairness financing involves sharing ownership and control of the business, which may limit decision-making liberty. By evaluating the danger visibility of various financing options, entrepreneurs can make informed choice that align with their danger permissiveness and overall business scheme. Another important factor to consider is the velocity and alleviate of obtaining financing. Depending on the urging of business need, entrepreneurs may need to explore alternative financing source that can provide financing quickly. Traditional bank may have lengthy coating process, whereas online lender or crowdfunding platform can offer faster access to uppercase. It is essential for entrepreneurs to assess their immediate and future financing requirement and choose a financing option that aligns with their timeline and availability requirement. Additionally, entrepreneurs should evaluate the effect of financing on their business's creditworthiness and future financing opportunities. Taking on debt can increase leverage ratio and affect recognition score, potentially limiting access to additional financing in the future. Entrepreneurs must carefully consider the long-term significance of financing decision and explore options that can enhance their financial believability and expand their borrow capability when needed. Entrepreneurs should assess the potential for external control or intervention when considering different financing options. Fairness financing, such as adventure uppercase or angel investing, often involves giving up partial ownership and may require sharing decision-making authorization with the investor. On the other paw, debt financing allows entrepreneurs to retain full ownership and control of the business but comes with the duty to repay to lend. Entrepreneurs must weigh the advantage and disadvantage of various financing options to determine which option best aligns with their entrepreneurial sight and personal preference. Entrepreneurs should critically evaluate the potential for long-term strategic partnership. While financing is primarily about uppercase extract, it can also present opportunities to establish partnership that go beyond financial support. Collaborative relationship with investor or lender who bring manufacture cognition, network, and expertness can support business increase and enlargement. Entrepreneurs should consider the intangible benefit that different financing options can provide, including access to mentorship, manufacture connection, and business developing opportunities. By evaluating these factor holistically, entrepreneurs can make informed decision about financing options that not only address their immediate uppercase need but also contribute to their long-term business sustainability and increase. One of the most important concept that entrepreneurs need to understand when it comes to finance is cash flow management. Cash flow refers to the movement of money into and out of a business, and it is essential for the endurance and growth of any adventure. Entrepreneurs should aim to have a positive cash flow, meaning that the inflows of cash from sale or investments exceed the outflows of cash for expenses or investments. Positive cash flow ensures that the business has enough money to cover its ongoing expenses and also allows for future investments or enlargement. On the other hand, negative cash flow can quickly lead to financial trouble and ultimately the loser of a business. There are several strategies that entrepreneurs can employ to effectively manage their cash flow and ensure its positive flight. First and foremost, entrepreneurs should establish a realistic cash flow forecast. A cash flow forecast is a forecast of the inflows and outflows of cash for a specific point, typically on a monthly fundament. By accurately predicting the next cash flows, entrepreneurs can plan accordingly and anticipate potential gap or surplus. These forecast should include the projected sale receipts, as well as the anticipated expenses such as lease, utility, salary, and other operational cost. It is crucial to be conservative in estimating the inflows and generous in projecting the outflows to account for any unexpected expenses or delay in receiving payments from customers. By having a comprehensive cash flow forecast, entrepreneurs can identify any potential issue ahead of clock and take appropriate action to mitigate them. Another effective scheme for cash flow management is to implement efficient payment terms and method. Entrepreneurs should strive to negotiate favorable payment terms with their supplier, such as longer payment period or discount for early payments. This will allow the business to hold onto their cash for a longer point and potentially earn more discount or concern income. On the other hand, entrepreneurs should assess their own payment terms with customers and consider implementing strict policy to ensure timely payments. This can be achieved through offering incentive for prompt payments or establishing penalty for late payments. By optimizing both the inflows and outflows of cash, entrepreneurs can maintain a healthy cash flow equilibrium. Entrepreneurs should proactively manage their working capital to enhance cash flow management. Working capital refers to the net fluid asset available for day-to-day operation, and it can heavily impact a business's cash flow. By carefully managing the level of inventorying, accounts receivable, and accounts payable, entrepreneurs can optimize their working capital and ensure a smooth cash flow. Maintaining a lean inventory and implementing just-in-time order can help reduce holding cost and free up cash. Additionally, closely monitoring accounts receivable and promptly following up with customers can accelerate cash inflows. Managing accounts payable carefully by negotiating payment terms and taking vantage of early payment discount can contribute to a positive cash flow. Cash flow management is a vital facet of financial management for entrepreneurs. It involves carefully monitoring the movement of money into and out of a business and ensuring a positive cash flow. To effectively manage cash flow, entrepreneurs should establish realistic cash flow forecast, negotiate favorable payment terms, and optimize their working capital. By implementing this strategy, entrepreneurs can maintain a healthy cash flow equilibrium and set their business up for long-term achiever and growth.

VI. COST ANALYSIS AND PRICING STRATEGIES

Understanding the costs associated with producing goods or services is crucial in determining the right pricing strategies to adopt. When conducting a cost analysis, entrepreneurs need to identify and evaluate both fixed and variable costs. Fixed costs refer to expense that do not change regardless of the level of production, such as lease and indemnity. On the other hand, variable costs are directly tied to the level of production and can include material, toil, and utility. By analyzing these costs, entrepreneurs can determine a break-even point, which is the level of production needed to cover all costs and begin generating profit. Once the costs have been analyzed, entrepreneurs can then move on to establishing pricing strategies. Pricing is a complex decision that requires careful circumstance of various factors, including costs, competition, and customer demand. There are several pricing strategies that entrepreneurs can choose from, including cost-plus pricing, market-based pricing, and value-based pricing. Cost-plus pricing involves adding a markup to the cost of producing the goods or services to determine the sell price. This strategy ensures that all costs are covered and allows for a desired profits' leeway to be achieved. It can be challenging to determine the appropriate markup that will make the product or service competitive in the market while still ensuring profitability. Market-based pricing, on the other hand, takes into account the prices of similar product or services in the market. By conducting market inquiry and studying competitor, entrepreneurs can set their prices based on what customers are willing to pay. This strategy requires a good understanding of the target market and the power to differentiate the product or service from competitor. Value-based pricing is a more customer-centric approach that focuses on the perceived value of the product or service. Entrepreneurs utilizing this strategy must determine the maximum price that customers are willing to pay based on the benefit they receive. This approach requires entrepreneurs to effectively communicate the value of their offer to customers and justify the higher price. Entrepreneurs should also consider the conception of price elasticity when determining pricing strategies. Price elasticity refer to the reactivity of customer demand to an altar in price. For instance, if a product is highly elastic, a small growth in price could result in a significant reduction in demand. On the other hand, if a product is inelastic, consumer are less likely to change their purchasing habit due to a price growth. By understanding the price elasticity of their product or service, entrepreneurs can make informed decisions regarding price change and promotion. In plus to these pricing strategies, entrepreneurs can also consider dynamic pricing, which involves adjusting prices based on real-time market weather. This approach is commonly used in industry such as airline, hotel, and e-commerce, where prices can fluctuate depending on factor such as demand, competition, and clock of buy. Dynamic pricing allows entrepreneurs to maximize receipts and profits by taking vantage of market fluctuation. Cost analysis and pricing strategies are important aspect of financial management for entrepreneurs. By conducting a thorough cost analysis, entrepreneurs can understand their expense and determine a break-even point. This info then serves as a groundwork for establishing pricing strategies that take into account costs, competition, and customer demand. Whether through cost-plus pricing, market-based pricing, or value-based pricing, entrepreneurs must choose a strategy that aligns with their clientele goal and target market. Additionally, considering price elasticity and dynamic pricing can further enhance the potency of pricing strategies. With a solid understanding of costs and pricing, entrepreneurs can make informed decisions to manage their finance and grow their business.

COST ANALYSIS IN DETERMINING PRODUCT/SERVICE PRICING

It allows entrepreneurs to understand the true cost of producing or providing their offering and enables them to make informed decisions regarding pricing strategies. By conducting a thorough cost analysis, entrepreneurs can effectively calculate the sum of receipts needed to cover all their costs and generate a reasonable profit margin. This knowledge is essential for sustaining a business in the long-running and ensuring its financial viability. Cost analysis provides entrepreneurs with insight into the profitability of different product line or services, allowing them to identify which aspects of their business are most profitable and which may need readjustment. Without a proper understanding of costs, entrepreneurs run the danger of underpricing their product or services, leading to financial loss and difficulty in achieving their desired profit goals. On the other paw, overpricing can also be detrimental, as it may discourage potential customers from making a buy. Cost analysis serves as a tool for assessing the efficiency and potency of business operations. Through analyzing costs, entrepreneurs can identify area where they can reduce expense and optimize resource allocation, thereby increasing the overall efficiency of their business. For instance, by identifying the most costly component of a product, entrepreneurs can explore opportunities for cost-saving, such as seeking alternative supplier or implementing procedure improvement. By doing so, entrepreneurs can enhance their competitive vantage by offering their product or service at a lower cost, while still maintaining a reasonable profit margin. Cost analysis can reveal the effect of economy of surmount, enabling entrepreneurs to determine the intensity of production or service proviso that would result in lower costs per unit. This knowledge is particularly beneficial for business that aspire to grow and expand their operations. By understanding the cost dynamic of their business, entrepreneurs can make informed decisions regarding enlargement strategies, such as entering new market or increasing production capability. Cost analysis plays a crucial part in pricing decisions for entrepreneurs operating in competitive market. Understanding the costs associated with their product or service allows entrepreneurs to determine the pricing threshold beyond which their offering becomes unattractive to potential customers. Additionally, cost analysis enables entrepreneurs to respond to pricing pressure imposed by competitors. By monitoring their costs, entrepreneurs can identify opportunities for cost reduction in reaction to aggressive pricing strategies from competitors. This proactive overture allows entrepreneurs to maintain fight while simultaneously safeguarding profitability. Importantly, cost analysis should not be viewed as a one-time exercising but as an ongoing procedure. Business weather may change over clock, and factor affecting costs, such as comment price or regulatory requirement, may fluctuate. Entrepreneurs must periodically review and update their cost analyses to ensure that their pricing remains accurate and aligned with their financial goals. Additionally, cost analysis can be extended beyond a basic understanding of production costs. Entrepreneurs can also consider other relevant costs, such as dispersion, merchandising, or customer acquirement expense, to gain a holistic perspective of cost structure. This comprehensive cost analysis provides entrepreneurs with a more accurate contemplation of the true costs associated with their product or service, enabling them to set price that are both fair to customers and profitable for their business. Cost analysis is of overriding grandness in determining product or service pricing for entrepreneurs. It facilitates informed decision-making, enables efficient resource allocation, enhances fight, and safeguard profitability. By conducting a thorough cost analysis, entrepreneurs can ensure that their pricing strategies align with their financial goals while remaining competitive in the marketplace. They can identify opportunities for cost reduction and area for business enlargement. Cost analysis serves as a vital tool for managing the financial aspects of a business and maximizing its long-term achiever.

TECHNIQUES FOR ACCURATELY CALCULATING COSTS: FIXED COSTS, VARIABLE COSTS, DIRECT COSTS AND INDIRECT COSTS

To effectively manage their money and grow their business, entrepreneurs need to understand and distinguish between various types of costs. These include fixed costs, variable costs, direct costs, and indirect costs. Fixed costs refer to expenses that do not change regardless of the level of production or sales. Example of fixed costs may include rent, salary, and indemnity premium. These costs are essential for the procedure of the business and are often incurred on a regular fundament. Variable costs, on the other hand, vacillate in ratio to the level of production or sales. These costs are directly tied to the intensity of commodity or services produced and include items such as raw materials, package, and direct toil. Understanding and accurately calculating variable costs is crucial for entrepreneurs as they can directly impact the profitability of the business. Direct costs are expenses that can be directly attributed to a specific product or service. These costs are incurred as a consequence of the production or deliverance of a particular item and can include materials, toil, and other associated expenses. By accurately calculating direct costs, entrepreneurs can determine the true cost of producing a product or service and set appropriate pricing. Indirect costs, on the other hand, are expenses that are not directly tied to a specific product or service but are necessary for the overall function of the business. These costs are often shared among multiple products or services and can include items such as utility, merchandising expenses, and administrative costs. Accurately calculating indirect costs allows entrepreneurs to allocate these expenses among different products or services and ensure that they are factored into the overall pricing scheme. For entrepreneurs, accurately calculating costs is not only crucial for financial plan and budget but also for making strategic business decisions. By understanding the different types of costs and how they affect the business, entrepreneurs can make informed decisions about pricing, production level, and resourcefulness allotment. By accurately calculating variable costs, entrepreneurs can determine the break-even level for their products or services. This is the level at which total sales receipts equal total costs and no profits or departure is made. Knowing the break-even level allows entrepreneurs to set sales target and make decisions about pricing and cost management. Additionally, understanding the different types of costs allows entrepreneurs to identify areas of high spending and explore opportunity for cost decrease and efficiency betterment. Accurately calculating costs also plays a crucial role in financial forecast and risk management. By having a clear understanding of the costs associated with their business, entrepreneurs can develop realistic financial projections and identify potential areas of financial risk. If variable costs are projected to increase due to change in raw material price, entrepreneurs can factor this info into their financial forecast and make adjustment to their pricing or cost management strategy. By accurately calculating costs, entrepreneurs can minimize the financial risk associated with unexpected cost fluctuation and ensure the long-term financial viability of their business. Accurate cost calculation is an essential facet of finance for entrepreneurs. Understanding and distinguishing between fixed costs, variable costs, direct costs, and indirect costs allows entrepreneurs to effectively manage their money and grow their business. By accurately calculating costs, entrepreneurs can make informed business decisions, set appropriate pricing, and develop realistic financial projections. Accurate cost calculation plays a crucial role in risk management and ensures the long-term financial viability of the business.

STRATEGIES FOR SETTING COMPETITIVE PRICES WHILE ENSURING PROFITABILITY

Strategies for setting competitive prices while ensuring profitability for a clientele necessitate careful circumstance and psychoanalysis. It is essential to strike an equilibrium between being competitive in the market and ensuring a reasonable profit margin. One strategy that entrepreneurs can utilize is cost-based pricing. This approach involves determining the costs incurred in producing a product or providing a service and adding a markup to cover both direct costs and overhead expense. By accurately calculating the costs and incorporating an appropriate profit margin, entrepreneurs can set prices that ensure profitability without sacrificing fight. Another strategy that entrepreneurs can employ is value-based pricing. This approach involves considering the perceived value that customers derive from a product or service and setting prices accordingly. By understanding customers' perception of value and positioning their offering accordingly, entrepreneurs can set prices that maximize profits while remaining competitive in the market. Another tactics that entrepreneurs can use is competitive pricing. This involves analyzing the pricing strategies of competitors and adjusting prices accordingly. If competitors are charging significantly lower prices for similar product or service, entrepreneurs may need to lower their prices to remain competitive. Conversely, if competitors are charging higher prices, entrepreneurs may have the chance to increase their prices while still attracting customers. Entrepreneurs can also consider implementing dynamic pricing strategies. This approach involves adjusting prices based on market conditions, such as requirement, inventorying level, or seasonal factor. By leveraging information and engineering, entrepreneurs can dynamically adjust prices to maximize profitability. For instance, an e-commerce retailer may lower prices during off-peak time to stimulate sale and increase receipts. Conversely, they may increase prices during high-demand period to capture additional profit. Additionally, entrepreneurs can consider promotional pricing as a strategy to both attract customers and maintain profitability. Temporary price reduction, discount, or bundled offer can be used to incentivize customers to choose their product or service over competitors. It is crucial to ensure that promotional pricing strategies are aligned with the overall profitability goal and are not eroding margin in the long-running. Entrepreneurs can also utilize price skimming or penetration pricing strategies. Price skimming involve initially setting high prices for innovative or unique product and gradually lowering them as competitor intensify or as new version of the product are released. This strategy allows entrepreneurs to maximize profit from early adopter while also capturing a larger market share over clock. On the other paw, penetration pricing involves setting low initial prices to quickly gain market share and attract customers. As the brand mark becomes established and customer allegiance is developed, entrepreneurs can gradually increase prices to ensure profitability. Setting competitive prices while ensuring profitability requires entrepreneurs to employ various strategies tailored to their specific clientele and market circumstance. By considering cost-based pricing, value-based pricing, competitive pricing, dynamic pricing, promotional pricing, and price skimming or penetration pricing, entrepreneurs can maximize their profits while remaining competitive. It is crucial for entrepreneurs to continuously monitor market conditions, competitors' pricing strategies, and customer perception to adjust their pricing strategies accordingly. As an entrepreneur, understanding how to manage finance is essential for the achiever and increase of your business. Financial management involves various activity, such as budgeting, forecasting, and analyzing financial statements, that play a crucial part in decision-making. One fundamental financial precept that entrepreneurs should grasp is the conception of cash flow. Cash flow represents the drift of money into and out of a business, and it is crucial for ensuring the steady operation of your venture. By monitoring and managing your cash flow effectively, you can avoid potential financial difficulties and maintain constancy. To begin, budgeting is a critical facet of financial management that helps entrepreneurs program and allocate their resource wisely. A budget is a detailed program that outlines the inflow and outflow of your business's fund over a specified point. It allows you to estimate your income and expenses accurately, ensuring that your revenues are sufficient to cover your cost. By creating a realistic budget, you can avoid overspending and identify potential area for price decrease. Additionally, monitoring your actual financial performance against your budget allows you to assess your business's financial wellness and make necessary adjustment. Forecasting is another essential instrument for entrepreneurs to manage their finance effectively. Forecasting involve estimating future financial outcome based on historical information and marketplace trend. By forecasting your revenues and expenses, you can anticipate potential change in your business's cash flow and make informed decisions accordingly. For instance, if your forecast indicates a potential reduction in sale, you can proactively adjust your expenses or seek additional financing to mitigate the impact. Conversely, if your forecast shows an increase chance, you can plan for enlargement or invest in new resource to seize that potential. Analyzing financial statements is a crucial accomplishment that entrepreneurs should develop to understand their business's financial performance. Financial statements, such as the income statement, equilibrium shroud, and cash flow statement, provide valuable insight into your business's revenue, expenses, asset, liability, and cash flow. By analyzing these statements, you can identify trend, compare your performance to manufacture benchmark, and make data-driven decisions. If your profits' leeway is declining, you can investigate the underlying cause and implement corrective action to improve profitability. Managing your cash flow effectively is vital for the financial sustainability of your business. Cash flow problem can arise when your expenses exceed your revenues, leading to challenge in meeting your financial obligation, such as paying supplier or employee. To manage your cash flow, you should monitor your receivables and payable diligently. Delayed client payment or extended recognition term granted to customer can impact your cash flow negatively. Similarly, postponing gender payment might strain your relationship and impact your purchasing force. By maintaining a robust cash flow, you can ensure that you have sufficient fund to cover your expenses and invest in future increase opportunity. Understanding fundamental financial principle and applying them to your business is crucial for entrepreneurs. By mastering financial management technique, such as budgeting, forecasting, and analyzing financial statements, you can make informed decisions that enhance your business's financial wellness. Paying particular care to cash flow management is vital for maintaining constancy and ensuring the steady operation of your venture. By implementing effective cash flow monitoring and management strategy, you can mitigate potential financial difficulties and stance your business for sustainable increase.

VII. CAPITAL BUDGETING AND INVESTMENT DECISIONS

Capital budgeting is a critical aspect of financial direction for entrepreneurs as it involves making strategic investment decisions that can significantly impact the long-term success of a business. This procedure involves evaluating potential investments and determining whether they are worth pursuing based on their expected returns and risks. By understanding the principles of capital budgeting, entrepreneurs can make informed decisions that maximize the value of their investments. One fundamental conception in capital budgeting is the time value of money. This principle recognizes that a dollar received in the future is worth less than a dollar received now due to the chance price of waiting. This means that the deserving of an investment is not solely based on its nominal value, but also on when the returns will be received. To account for this, entrepreneurs use various techniques, such as discounted cash flow analysis, to estimate the present value of future cash flows. By discounting future cash flows, entrepreneurs can compare investments with different time and select the single that offers the highest net present value. Another important aspect of capital budgeting is assessing the risk associated with an investment. Risk refer to the incertitude of achieving the expected returns from an investment. Entrepreneurs must consider both the systematic risk, which is the market-wide risk that cannot be diversified away, and the non-systematic risk, which is unique to a specific investment and can be reduced through variegation. To evaluate the risk of an investment, entrepreneurs use various techniques, such as sensitiveness analysis and scenario analysis, to assess the impact of different factor on the investment's expected returns. By understanding the risk-return tradeoff, entrepreneurs can determine whether an investment's potential returns justify its risks. Entrepreneurs need to consider the impact of taxes on investment decisions. Taxes can significantly affect the profitability of an investment by reducing the net cash flows received. To account for taxes, entrepreneurs use techniques such as after-tax analysis and tax shields. After-tax analysis involves adjusting the expected cash flows for taxes to accurately estimate the investment's net present value. Additionally, tax shields, such as derogation and concern disbursement deduction, can reduce the taxable income and consequence in lower tax liability, increasing the investment's profitability. By considering the tax significance, entrepreneurs can make more accurate investment decisions and maximize their after-tax returns. Entrepreneurs must consider the impact of incertitude and tractability on investment decisions. The business surroundings are dynamic and can change rapidly, leading to unforeseen opportunity or risks. Entrepreneurs should evaluate investments with tractability in psyche. Real option analysis is a technique that incorporates the value of tractability into investment decisions. It recognizes that some investments provide the correct but not the duty to take vantage of future opportunity. By valuing these option, entrepreneurs can make better investment decisions in uncertain environment. Capital budgeting is a crucial procedure for entrepreneurs as it involves making strategic investment decisions that can significantly impact the long-term success of a business. By understanding the principles of capital budgeting, entrepreneurs can make informed decisions that maximize the value of their investments. Key concept in capital budgeting include the time value of money, risk appraisal, tax consideration, and incertitude analysis. By incorporating these factor into their investment decisions, entrepreneurs can increase the likeliness of achieving their financial goal and growing their business successfully.

DEFINITION AND SIGNIFICANCE OF CAPITAL BUDGETING

Capital budgeting refer to the procedure through which businesses determine which investment projects to undertake in ordering to allocate their limited financial resources optimally. It involves evaluating potential investment and determining their feasibility and profitability in the long-running. The meaning of capital budgeting lies in its ability to guide entrepreneurs in making crucial financial decisions that can have a substantial effect on the success or loser of their businesses. One of the primary reason why capital budgeting holds immense grandness is its role in maximizing a company's return on investment (ROI) . By carefully evaluating various investment options and selecting those that promise the highest potential return, entrepreneurs can ensure that their resources are allocated in the most effective and efficient way. This, in turn, helps them generate higher profit and enhance stockholder valuate. In plus to ROI, capital budgeting also helps entrepreneurs identify potential risk associated with investment projects. By conducting detailed danger assessment, businesses can gain a better understand of the potential pitfall and develop strategy to mitigate them, thereby minimizing potential losses. Capital budgeting plays a pivotal role in strategic decision-making. By thoroughly evaluating investment opportunities and aligning them with the company's overall goal and objectives, entrepreneurs can make informed decisions that are in pipeline with their long-term strategic plan. This enables them to prioritize investment that are crucial for achieving their business objectives, such as expanding into new market, introducing new product, or enhancing their competitive stance. Without capital budgeting, entrepreneurs may make impulsive or uninformed investment decisions, which could lead to wasteful expenditure or missed opportunities for increase and enlargement. Capital budgeting facilitate effective resource allotment and budgeting. By systematically evaluating different investment options, businesses can allocate their financial resources in a way that optimizes their usage. Capital budgeting helps entrepreneurs identify projects that require significant amount of capital investment and may require long-term funding options, such as deposit loan or fairness investment. By planning for this financial need in advanced, entrepreneurs can secure the necessary fund and avoid potential liquid issue or delay in project execution. Additionally, capital budgeting allows businesses to prioritize projects based on their urging and grandness, ensuring that the limited resources are allocated to the most critical projects first. Another crucial facet of capital budgeting is its ability to provide a framework for measuring and monitoring the performance of investment projects. By establishing relevant performance metric, entrepreneurs can regularly evaluate the progression and success of ongoing projects. This enables them to make timely adjustment or take corrective action if projects are not performing as expected, thereby minimizing potential losses. The measuring and monitoring of investment project performance service as a valuable feedback mechanics for entrepreneurs, allowing them to learn from experience and refine their next investment decisions. Capital budgeting is an essential financial instrument that helps entrepreneurs make informed investment decisions and allocate their resources optimally. Its meaning lies in its ability to maximize return on investment, facilitate strategic decision-making, supporting effective resource allotment, and provide a framework for measuring and monitoring project performance. By utilizing capital budgeting technique, entrepreneurs can mitigate risk, seize opportunities for increase, and ultimately enhance the financial wellness and success of their businesses. It is imperative for entrepreneurs to grasp the gist of capital budgeting and apply it diligently to ensure the long-term sustainability and profitability of their venture.

TECHNIQUES FOR EVALUATING INVESTMENT OPPORTUNITIES: PAYBACK PERIOD, NET PRESENT VALUE AND INTERNAL RATE OF RETURN

Another technique for evaluating investment opportunities is the payback period. The payback period is the sum of time it takes for an investment to recover its initial cost or investment. It is calculated by dividing the initial cost of the investment by the annual cash inflows. The shorter the payback period, the more attractive the investment opportunity is considered to be. The payback period does not take into account the time value of money and does not consider cash flows beyond the payback period. The net present value (NPV) is another widely used technique for evaluating investment opportunities. NPV is the divergence between the present value of cash inflows and the present value of cash outflow over the life of the investment. It takes into account the time value of money by discounting future cash flows back to their present value using a discount rate. If the NPV is positive, the investment is considered to be profitable. Conversely, if the NPV is negative, the investment is considered to be unprofitable. The higher the NPV, the more attractive the investment opportunity is considered to be. The internal rate of return (IRR) is a technique used to evaluate the potential profitability of an investment opportunity. The IRR is the discount rate that makes the net present value of the investment equal to zero. In other phrase, it is the rate at which the investment break even. If the IRR is higher than the required rate of return or the hurdle rate, the investment is considered to be profitable. Conversely, if the IRR is lower than the required rate of return, the investment is considered to be unprofitable. The IRR is a useful technique as it takes into account the time value of money and provides a single rate of return that allows for easy comparing of different investment opportunities. When evaluating investment opportunities, it is important to consider the strengths and limitation of each technique. The payback period is a simple and easy to understand technique, but it does not consider the time value of money and ignores cash flows beyond the payback period. The net present value takes into account the time value of money and consider cash flows over the life of the investment, but it requires the decision of an appropriate discount rate. The internal rate of return also takes into account the time value of money and provides a single rate of return for comparing, but it can be difficult to calculate and interpret. It is also important to consider other factors and qualitative information when evaluating investment opportunities. These may include the potential risk and uncertainty associated with the investment, the strategic fit with the clientele, the potential effect on the party's operation and financial execution, and the potential for future increase and enlargement. It is crucial to take a comprehensive and holistic overture to evaluating investment opportunities, considering both quantitative and qualitative factors, in ordering to make well-informed investment decisions. There are various technique available to evaluate investment opportunities, including the payback period, net present value, and internal rate of return. Each technique has its own strengths and limitation and should be used in conjunctive with other factors and qualitative information when making investment decisions. By utilizing this technique effectively, entrepreneur can make informed decisions and maximize the profitability and increase potential of their business.

FACTORS TO CONSIDER WHEN MAKING INVESTMENT DECISIONS FOR BUSINESS GROWTH

When it comes to making investment decisions for business growth, entrepreneurs need to carefully consider several factors in ordering to make informed choice that will lead to successful outcome. One crucial factor to consider is the overall economic environment in which the business operates. Entrepreneurs should evaluate the current commonwealth of the thriftiness, including factors such as concern rates, ostentatiousness, and overall market weather. By doing so, entrepreneurs can identify whether it is a favorable clock to invest and determine the potential risks and reward associated with their investment decisions. Another important factor to consider is the specific industry in which the business operates. Dissimilar industry have varying level of fight, growth potential, and market dynamic. Entrepreneurs need to conduct thorough inquiry and analysis to gain a deep understanding of the industry they are operating in. This includes evaluating market trends, competitive landscape, industry regulation, and barrier to entering. By understanding the unique characteristic of their industry, entrepreneurs can make more informed investment decisions that align with the specific need and challenge of their business. Additionally, entrepreneurs should assess the financial wellness and execution of their own business before making investment decisions. This includes analyzing key financial metric such as receipts growth, profitability, cash flowing, and debt level. By evaluating the financial potency of their business, entrepreneurs can determine whether they have the resource and capability to fund investments and sustain growth in the long condition. They should also consider the potential affect that investments may have on their financial position, such as increased debt or dilution of possession. It is essential to strike an equilibrium between investing in growth opportunities and maintaining a healthy financial position. Alongside evaluating their own business, entrepreneurs should also assess their competitors and the broader market. This involves conducting a competitive analysis to understand the strength, weakness, and strategy of their competitors. By gaining insight into their competitors' investments and growth strategy, entrepreneurs can identify potential opportunities for their own business. Additionally, entrepreneurs should analyze market trends and client preference to identify emerging growth opportunities and potential threat. By staying ahead of market trends, entrepreneurs can position their business for achiever and make investment decisions that will help them take vantage of market opportunities. Risk appraisal is another critical factor to consider when making investment decisions. Every investment carries a certain tier of risk, and entrepreneurs need to carefully evaluate the potential risks and their permissiveness for risk. This includes conducting a thorough analysis of both financial and non-financial risks. Financial risks may include factors such as market unpredictability, concern rate fluctuation, or change in client requirement. Non-financial risks may include factors such as regulatory change, technological advancement, or supplying string disruption. By understanding the potential risks associated with their investments, entrepreneurs can develop strategy to mitigate those risks and make informed decisions that align with their risk permissiveness. When making investment decisions for business growth, entrepreneurs need to carefully consider several factors. These include evaluating the overall economic environment, understanding the specific industry dynamic, assessing the financial wellness of their own business, analyzing competitors and market trends, and conducting a thorough risk appraisal. By taking these factors into calculate, entrepreneurs can make informed investment decisions that will contribute to the successful growth and long-term sustainability of their business. One of the most fundamental financial principle that entrepreneurs must understand and apply to their business is the concept of cash flow management. Cash flow refers to the movement of money into and out of a business, and it is crucial for the endurance and growth of any adventure. Effective cash flow management involves monitor and controlling the inflow and outflow of cash to ensure that there is enough available to cover expenses and meet financial obligation. Entrepreneurs need to have a clear understanding of their cash flow position, including sources of cash influx, such as sale receipts or investments, and sources of cash leakage, such as expenses and lend repayment. By forecasting and monitor cash flow, entrepreneurs can identify potential cash shortage in advanced and take necessary action to mitigate them. One key aspect of cash flow management is understanding and managing the timing of cash flows. In many businesses, there can be significant delay between the time a sale is made, and the time cash is received. This is especially true for business that offer recognition to customer, where payment may not be received until week or even month after the sale. It is essential for entrepreneurs to be aware of these timing divergence and program accordingly.

They may need to implement strategy to accelerate cash inflow, such as offering discount for early payment or tightening recognition term. At the same time, they should also aim to delay cash outflow as much as possible, such as negotiating favorable payment term with supplier or using recognition facility wisely. Another important precept for entrepreneurs to understand is the concept of profitability and its kinship to cash flow. Profitability refers to the ability of a business to generate an excess after deducting all expenses from receipts, while cash flow refers to the actual movement of cash in and out of the business. Although profitability is a crucial long-term finish for any business, it is possible for a profitable business to experience short-term cash flow challenge. For instance, a business may have significant upfront cost or confront delay in receiving payment, which can lead to negative cash flow even if the business is ultimately profitable. Entrepreneurs must, therefore, closely monitor both profitability and cash flow to ensure the overall financial health of their business. Dealing with financial uncertainty and danger is another critical aspect of financial management for entrepreneurs. Running any business involves inherent uncertainty, such as fluctuating client requirement, changing marketplace weather, or unforeseen expenses. Entrepreneurs must be prepared for this uncertainty and have contingency in spot. Building up a cash stockpile or accessing line of recognition can provide a safe earnings during time of unexpected expenses or low cash flow. Regular financial psychoanalysis and scenario plan can also help entrepreneurs identify and address potential risk to their business. Understanding the part of financing and capital structure is vital for entrepreneurs. Financing refers to the various way entrepreneurs can obtain fund to support their business activity, such as through loan, fairness investments, or retained profits. The selection of financing can significantly impact the financial health and growth possible of a business. Entrepreneurs must carefully evaluate the cost and benefit of different financing option and consider factor such as concern rate, refund term, and the effect on possession and command. They should also assess the optimal capital structure for their business, which refers to the mixture of debt and fairness financing. Achieving an optimal capital structure can help entrepreneurs secure adequate financing while minimizing financial danger and maximizing the rejoin on investment. Understanding fundamental financial principle and how to apply them to their business is crucial for entrepreneurs. Cash flow management, timing of cash flows, profitability, dealing with uncertainty and danger, and financing and capital structure are all key component of effective financial management. By applying this principle, entrepreneurs can make informed financial decision and ensure the long-term achiever and growth of their business.

VIII. RISK MANAGEMENT AND INSURANCE

Proper risk management is essential for entrepreneurs in ordering to protect their business from unforeseen event and potential liabilities. Risk management involves identifying potential risks, evaluating their potential impact, and implementing strategies to mitigate or transfer these risks. One important facet of risk management is insurance, which provides financial protection against various types of risks. There are several types of insurance that entrepreneurs should consider for their business, including property insurance, liability insurance, and key person insurance. Property insurance is essential for business that own or lease physical asset, such as building, equipment, or inventorying. This type of insurance provides coverage against damage or loss due to event such as burn, larceny, or natural disaster. By having property insurance, entrepreneurs can transfer the risk of potential losses to an insurance party, helping to protect their investing and ensuring business persistence in the issue of an unforeseen incidental. Liability insurance is another important type of insurance for entrepreneurs. It provides coverage against potential legal claims and liabilities that may arise from the operation of a business. This can include situation where a client is injured on the business premise, or where the business is found to be legally liable for damage caused to a third company. Liability insurance helps protect entrepreneurs from potentially significant financial losses due to legal expense, settlement, or judgment that may arise from such claims. In plus to property and liability insurance, entrepreneurs should also consider key person insurance. This type of insurance provides coverage for the loss of a key employee or father of the business. In many small businesses, the success and profitability of the business heavily rely on the cognition, skill, and relationship of key individual. Key person insurance provides financial protection in the issue that a key person becomes disabled or passes away. The insurance continue can be used to cover the cost associated with find and training a replacing, as well as to compensate for the loss of key client or business opportunity that may result from the absence of the key person. While insurance is an important component of risk management, it is not the only instrument entrepreneurs have at their disposition. There are other risk management strategies that entrepreneurs can employ to minimize the potential impact of risks on their business. One such scheme is to implement effective internal controls and procedure to reduce the likeliness of fraudulence, mistake, or other operational risks. By having proper procedure in spot, entrepreneurs can mitigate the risk of financial losses and ensure the truth and completeness of their financial record. Additionally, variegation is another risk management scheme that entrepreneurs can use to mitigate the impact of risks. By diversifying their source of receipts, product, or client ground, entrepreneurs can reduce their dependency on a single generator of income or marketplace section. This can help to minimize the potential impact of any adverse event or change in marketplace weather that may affect one particular region of the business. Risk management and insurance play a critical part in protecting entrepreneurs and their business from potential financial losses and liabilities. By identifying and evaluating potential risks, entrepreneurs can implement strategies to mitigate or transfer these risks. Insurance provides financial protection against various types of risks, such as property damage or legal claims. Entrepreneurs should also consider other risk management strategies, such as effective internal controls and variegation, to minimize the potential impact of risks on their business. By adopting a comprehensive risk management overture, entrepreneurs can ensure the long-term success and increase of their business.

RISK MANAGEMENT FOR ENTREPRENEURS

As innovator and creator, entrepreneurs often have a higher permissiveness for risk compared to traditional business owner. This does not mean that they are immune to the potential negative consequence that arise from taking risks. In fact, it is crucial for entrepreneurs to understand the significance of risk management and actively incorporate it into their decision-making processes in ordering to maximize their chance of achiever. One of the primary reason why risk management is essential for entrepreneurs is the security it provides against potential financial losses. Starting and running a business involves a significant investing of uppercase, and entrepreneurs often put their personal saving or seek external financing to finance their venture. The consequence of a financial loss can be detrimental not only to the business but also to the entrepreneur's personal financial constancy. By implementing risk management practices, entrepreneurs can identify potential threats and implement strategies to mitigate them. This can include to utilize of indemnity to protect against unpredictable event, variegation of receipts stream to reduce trust on a single generator of income, and regularly monitoring financial statement to identify potential risks early on. Risk management allows entrepreneurs to make informed and calculated decisions. When faced with incertitude or the chance to take a risk, entrepreneurs can rely on risk management principle to assess the potential outcome and weigh the reward against the potential losses. By thoroughly evaluating the risks and reward associated with each decision, entrepreneurs can make strategic choice that align with their overall goal and objective. This can help them avoid overhasty or impulsive decisions that may have detrimental effect on their business in the long-running. Another crucial facet of risk management for entrepreneurs is its affect on a business's reputation and customer trust. In an increasingly interconnected and transparent globe, tidings of a business loser or outrage spread rapidly, potentially leading to a loss of reputation and customer allegiance. By implementing risk management measure, entrepreneurs can identify potential threats to their reputation, such as unethical practices or merchandise recall, and take proactive step to minimize their happening. This can include implementing internal control and monitoring system, conducting regular risk assessment, and ensuring compliance with legal and ethical standard. By actively managing these risks, entrepreneurs can safeguard their businesses and maintain the trust and trust of their customer and stakeholder. Risk management enables entrepreneurs to seize opportunities and innovate without compromising the long-term sustainability of their businesses. Risk and opportunities often go paw in paw, and entrepreneurs must be able to assess and manage both effectively. By embracing risk management practices, entrepreneurs can identify and evaluate potential opportunities, make informed decisions about whether to pursue them, and develop strategies to mitigate associated risks. This can give entrepreneurs a competitive boundary in the marketplace by allowing them to capitalize on emerging trend, new technology, or untapped customer segment. Risk management is of utmost importance for entrepreneurs as they navigate the challenge and uncertain landscape of business. By implementing risk management practices, entrepreneurs can protect themselves against financial losses, make informed decisions, safeguard their reputation and customer trust, and seize opportunities for increase and invention. Given the inherent risks involved in entrepreneurship, it is essential for entrepreneurs to understand the significance of risk management and actively incorporate it into their decision-making processes to ensure the long-term achiever and sustainability of their businesses.

TYPES OF RISKS FACED BY BUSINESSES: OPERATIONAL, FINANCIAL, MARKET, ETC.

Businesses face various type of risks that can impact their operation and financial performance. One major type of risk is operational risk, which refers to the potential for loss due to inadequate or failed internal process, system, or human mistake. This can include risks associated with supplying string disruption, equipment loser, employee wrongdoing, or even natural disaster. Operational risks can significantly impact a business's power to deliver products or services, manage client relationship, and maintain profitability. It is crucial for entrepreneurs to identify and mitigate these risks through effective risk management strategies and eventuality plan. Financial risk is another significant type of risk that businesses face. This encompasses the potential for financial loss or incertitude arising from a company's investment, funding activities, or overall financial construction. For instance, businesses may face risks related to currency fluctuation, interest rate unpredictability, or changes in market conditions that affect to valuate of their investment or price of uppercase. Additionally, high level of debt or trust on specific source of financing can create financial risk, as the unfitness to meet financial obligation can lead to failure or other severe consequence. To manage financial risk, entrepreneurs need to assess their business's financial stance, maintain a diversified investing portfolio, and develop appropriate financial strategies, such as hedging against currency or interest rate risks. Market risk is another critical type of risk that businesses must navigate. Market risk refers to the potential for loss due to adverse changes in market conditions, including fluctuation in requirement, competitive pressure, or changes in consumer preference. Businesses face market risk when they are exposed to a highly competitive market, rely on a specific client section or dispersion canal, or operate in a rapidly changing manufacture. Adapting to market changes and staying ahead of competitor are essential for businesses to remain relevant and successful. Entrepreneurs can mitigate market risks by conducting comprehensive market inquiry, diversifying their client ground, and continually monitoring market trend to identify new opportunity and adjust business strategies accordingly. Effectual and regulatory risks are significant concern for businesses, particularly those operating in highly regulated industry or across international border. Non-compliance with laws and regulation can expose businesses to legal activity, fine, reputational harm, or even loss of operational license. Entrepreneurs must understand and comply with applicable laws and regulation to minimize these risks. This may involve obtaining legal pleader, implementing internal control, and conducting regular audit to ensure compliance. Businesses also face reputational risk, which is the potential for harm to a company's repute or brand mark picture. Reputational risk can arise from negative client experience, product recall, ethical controversy, or poor management decision. A damaged repute can lead to a loss of client confidence, decreased sale, and trouble attracting and retaining top endowment. Entrepreneurs must prioritize construction and maintaining a positive repute by delivering high-quality products or services, practicing ethical business behavior, and promptly addressing any issue or concern raised by customer. Businesses face an array of risks that can impact their operation, financial performance, and overall achiever. Operating, financial, market, legal, and reputational risks are among the key risks entrepreneurs must understand and manage. By implementing effective risk management strategies, diversifying their business activities, and staying vigilant to market changes and legal requirement, entrepreneurs are better positioned to navigate the complex landscape of risks and sustain long-term business increase.

STRATEGIES FOR MITIGATING RISKS AND THE ROLE OF INSURANCE IN RISK MANAGEMENT

Entrepreneurs face numerous uncertainty and potential setback, ranging from market unpredictability and economic downturn to legal challenges and operational disruptions. Having a clear scheme for risk management is crucial to ensure the long-term viability and sustainability of a business. This paragraph aims to explore different strategy that entrepreneurs can employ to mitigate risks and the critical role that insurance plays in this procedure. One of the primary strategy for managing risks is variegation. By spreading their investment across various assets, industries, or geographic region, entrepreneurs can limit the impact of a single risk event on their overall portfolio. Variegation provides a safe earnings by reducing the correlation between different investing option, thereby cushioning the negative effect of downside risks. A business owner can diversify their receipts stream by expanding into related market or targeting different client segment. This not only helps to mitigate risks associated with change in consumer preference but also provides opportunity for increase and expanding market deal. In the circumstance of investing, entrepreneurs can diversify their financial portfolio by investing in a mixture of stock, bond, commodity, or real demesne. This ensures that fluctuation in one asset grade do not have a significant adverse impact on the overall investing execution. Another effective risk mitigation scheme is proactive risk assessment and planning. By identifying and analyzing potential risks in advanced, entrepreneurs can develop eventuality plan and implement preventive measures to minimize their impact. This involves conducting thorough risk assessments, regularly monitoring market trends, and staying informed about industry-specific challenges and opportunity. A business owner can anticipate operational disruptions by investing in robust IT substructure, implementing redundancy plan, and establishing collaboration network with supplier and partner in different geographical location. Similarly, entrepreneurs can evaluate their business construction and identify potential legal risks by working closely with legal expert and ensuring compliance with relevant regulation and manufacture standard. Insurance plays a crucial role in risk management by transferring a component of the financial onus associated with potential risks to an insurance supplier. Insurance policies, such as property insurance, liability insurance, and business interruption insurance, offer entrepreneurs security against various contingency. Property insurance provides reportage for physical assets, such as building, equipment, and inventorying, against risks like burn, larceny, or natural disaster. Liability insurance protect business from potential lawsuit and claim arising from accident, merchandise defect, or professional error. Business interruption insurance compensates entrepreneurs for the departure of income when operation are disrupted due to unforeseen event, such as a pandemic or a major supplying string disruption. By transferring the financial risks to an insurance party, entrepreneurs can mitigate the potential adverse impact of these risks on their business operation and financial constancy. Effective risk management is a critical facet of running a successful business. Entrepreneurs can employ various strategy to mitigate risks, including variegation and proactive risk assessment and planning. Variegation helps to spread investment and receipts source across different assets or industries, reducing the impact of a single risk event. Proactive risk assessment and planning involve conducting thorough risk assessments, monitoring market trends, and implementing preventive measures. Additionally, insurance plays a vital role in risk management by transferring financial risks to insurance provider. Insurance policies compensate entrepreneurs for potential loss associated with property harm, liability claim, and business interruption. By employing this strategy and utilizing insurance as a risk mitigation instrument, entrepreneurs can enhance their business's resiliency and long-term prospect. Financial management plays a crucial part in the success and growth of any business, especially for entrepreneurs. Understanding fundamental financial principles and knowing how to apply them effectively can make or break a business venture. One of the key aspect of financial management is managing cash flow. Entrepreneurs must effectively manage their cash flow to ensure that there is enough money coming in to cover expenses and invest in growth opportunity. This requires careful plan and monitor of income and expenses. By keeping a closing eyeball on cash flow, entrepreneurs can make informed decisions about when to make purchase, negotiate favorable term with supplier, and even invest in new product or service. In plus to managing cash flow, entrepreneurs must also have a solid understanding of budgeting. An effective budget serve as a roadmap for the business, outlining expected revenue and expenses, and allowing entrepreneurs to plan for both the short and long term. By budgeting effectively, entrepreneurs can identify area where they can reduce cost, allocate resources efficiently, and make informed decisions about their business. Financial management also involves managing debt and capital. Many entrepreneurs rely on loan and other form of funding to start or expand their business. While debt can be a useful instrument for growth, it also carries risks. It is crucial for entrepreneurs to carefully consider their borrow option and think about the long-term significance of taking on debt. By understanding the different funding option available and evaluating the cost and benefit, entrepreneurs can make informed decisions about how to best manage their debt and capital. This includes not only managing existing debt but also planning for future financing need. Effective financial management also involves knowing how to analyze and interpret financial statements. These statements provide valuable insight into the financial health and execution of the business. Entrepreneurs should be able to read financial statements, such as the equilibrium shroud, income statement, and cash flow statement, and use them to make informed decisions. By analyzing financial statements, entrepreneurs can identify trend, supervise key execution indicator, and evaluate the overall financial health of their business. This knowledge is essential for identifying area for betterment, assessing the effect of decisions, and making strategic business decisions. Financial management also requires effective risk management. Entrepreneurship is inherently risky, and entrepreneurs must be prepared to deal with potential risks and uncertainty. This involves identifying and evaluating potential risks, such as change in the marketplace, client preference, or regulatory surroundings. Entrepreneurs should have eventuality plan in spot to mitigate these risks and ensure the long-term sustainability of their business. This includes having appropriate indemnity reportage, establishing exigency fund, and diversifying sources of receipts. By effectively managing risks, entrepreneurs can minimize their potential affect and stance their business for long-term success. Financial management is a critical accomplishment for entrepreneurs to maestro. By understanding fundamental financial principles and applying them effectively, entrepreneurs can make informed decisions, improve cash flow, allocate resources efficiently, and manage risks effectively. This knowledge and accomplishment set can make a significant divergence in the success and growth of a business venture. Whether it is managing cash flow, budgeting effectively, managing debt and capital, analyzing financial statements, or managing risks, entrepreneurs must be equipped with the necessary financial management skill to navigate the complex globe of business finance.

IX. FINANCIAL RATIOS AND PERFORMANCE ANALYSIS

Financial ratios are an essential instrument for entrepreneurs to evaluate the financial health and performance of their businesses. These ratios provide insights into various aspects of a company's operations, such as profitability, liquid, solvency, and efficiency. By analyzing these ratios, entrepreneurs can identify areas in which their businesses are excelling and areas that require improvement. One important financial ratio is the gross profit leeway, which measures the profitability of a company's nucleus operations. It is calculated by subtracting the cost of goods sold from net sales and dividing the consequence of net sales. A high gross profit leeway indicates that a business is generating sufficient receipts to cover its direct cost and have a profit leave over. Conversely, a low gross profit leeway suggests that a company may be selling its product or service at a cost that does not adequately cover its cost. Entrepreneurs can use this ratio to assess the price scheme of their businesses and make adjustment if necessary. Another crucial ratio for entrepreneurs is the current ratio, which measures a company's liquid or its power to meet short-term obligation. It is calculated by dividing current asset by current liability. A current ratio of less than 1 indicates that a company may struggle to meet its immediate financial obligation, while a ratio greater than 1 suggests that it has sufficient resource to do so. Monitoring the current ratio is vital for entrepreneurs to ensure that their businesses can meet their day-to-day expense and maintain a healthy cash flow. Debt ratio is a financial ratio that indicates the ratio of a company's asset financed by debt. It is calculated by dividing total debt by total asset. A high debt ratio poses a higher danger for a company as it indicates a heavy trust on debt to fund its operations. Entrepreneurs should strive to keep their businesses' debt within a reasonable array to avoid potential financial suffering. By analyzing the debt ratio, entrepreneurs can understand the extent to which their businesses are financed by debt and make informed decisions regarding their uppercase construction. Efficiency ratios, such as the inventory turnover ratio and the accounts receivable turnover ratio, bill how effectively a company manages its asset and converts them into sales and cash. The inventory turnover ratio is calculated by dividing the cost of goods sold by the average inventory valuate. This ratio indicates how quickly a company sells its inventory and replenishes it. A high inventory turnover ratio is desirable as it suggests efficient inventory direction and minimizes the danger of inventory obsolescence. The accounts receivable turnover ratio, on the other paw, measures how quickly a company collects outstanding client payment. It is calculated by dividing net recognition sales by average accounts receivable. A high accounts receivable turnover ratio indicates an efficient collecting procedure and a healthy cash flow. In plus to these ratios, entrepreneurs should also consider benchmarking their businesses against manufacture standard and competitor to gain a broader view on their performance. This can help identify areas of potency and weakness relative to peer and provide insights for improvement. Financial ratios and performance psychoanalysis are indispensable tool for entrepreneurs to effectively manage their businesses. By understanding and utilizing these ratios, entrepreneurs can gain valuable insights into their company' financial health and performance. Armed with this cognition, they can make informed decisions, implement effective strategy, and drive their businesses towards increase and achiever.

KEY FINANCIAL RATIOS: LIQUIDITY RATIOS, PROFITABILITY RATIOS AND EFFICIENCY RATIOS

Liquidity ratios, profitability ratios, and efficiency ratios are key financial ratios that help entrepreneurs gain valuable insights into the financial wellness and performance of their business. Liquidity ratios are primarily concerned with assessing a company's ability to meet its short-term financial obligations. One commonly used liquidity ratio is the current ratio, which is calculated by dividing current assets by current liabilities. This ratio indicates whether a company has enough short-term assets to cover its immediate liabilities. A current ratio of 2 or higher is generally considered favorable, as it implies that a company has enough resource to meet its short-term obligations. Another important liquidity ratio is the quick ratio, also known as the acid-test ratio. It measures a company's ability to pay off its current liabilities with its most liquid assets, excluding inventory. A quick ratio of 1 or higher is generally considered nonpareil. Profitability ratios, as the epithet suggests, focus on evaluating a company's profitability and its ability to generate profits from its operations. Gross profit margin, for instance, measures the percentage of sales revenue that remains after subtracting the cost of goods sold. It is calculated by dividing gross profit by sales revenue and multiplying the consequence of 100. A higher gross profit margin indicates that a company has a better command over its output cost and is more efficient at generating profits. Net profit margin, on the other paw, measures the percentage of sales revenue that remains after subtracting all expense, including tax and concern. This ratio provides a broader photograph of a company's overall profitability. A higher net profit margin indicates that a company is able to generate more profits from its sales. Efficiency ratios, also known as activeness ratios, assess how effectively a company utilizes its assets to generate sales revenue. One commonly used efficiency ratio is the asset turnover ratio, which measures how efficiently a company uses its total assets to generate sales. It is calculated by dividing sales revenue by total assets. A higher asset turnover ratio implies that a company is making efficient utilize of its assets to generate sales. Another efficiency ratio is the inventory turnover ratio, which measures the amount of time a company's inventory is sold and replaced during a specific point. It is calculated by dividing cost of goods sold by average inventory. A higher inventory turnover ratio suggests that a company is selling its inventory quickly, which is generally seen as positive. It indicates that the company is avoiding excess inventory and possibly maximizing its profits. By regularly analyzing these key financial ratios, entrepreneurs can gain valuable insights into the financial performance of their business. Liquidity ratios provide an understanding of the company's short-term financial wellness, helping entrepreneurs assess their ability to meet their short-term obligations. Profitability ratios help entrepreneurs assess the company's ability to generate profits from its operations, allowing them to make informed decision about price strategy and cost direction. Efficiency ratios enable entrepreneurs to evaluate the company's operational efficiency and make adjustment to improve productiveness and potency. Understanding and applying these key financial ratios is crucial for entrepreneurs to manage their money and grow their business successfully. By monitoring these ratios over clock and comparing them to manufacture benchmark, entrepreneurs can identify area of betterment and take appropriate action to enhance their financial performance. Regular financial ratio psychoanalysis can also provide early warn sign of financial suffering and help entrepreneurs proactively address potential issue before they escalate. The usage of these key financial ratios empower entrepreneurs to make informed financial decision and ultimately contributes to the long-term achiever of their business.

FINANCIAL RATIOS IN ASSESSING BUSINESS PERFORMANCE

Financial ratios offers valuable insights into various aspects of a company's financial health. These ratios enable entrepreneurs and investors to evaluate a company's profitability, liquidity, solvency, and efficiency, providing a comprehensive overview that can inform critical business decisions. Profitability ratios such as return on assets (ROA) , return on fairness (ROE) , and gross profit leeway (GPM) bill a company's ability to generate profit relative to its assets, fairness, and receipts, respectively. By analyzing these ratios, entrepreneurs can gauge how effectively their business is utilizing its resource and compare their performance to industry benchmark. Liquidity ratios like the current ratio and quick ratio assess a company's short-term financial health by examining its ability to meet its current obligations. These ratios serve as indicator of a company's liquidity stance and its capability to handle immediate financial demand or unexpected economic downturn. Additionally, solvency ratios, such as the debt-to-equity ratio and concern reportage ratio, evaluate a company's long-term financial constancy and its ability to meet long-term debt obligations. These ratios are crucial for entrepreneurs seeking to understand their business's financial leveraging and potential risk associated with excessive debt. Efficiency ratios, including inventorying turnover, receivables turnover, and asset turnover, bill how efficiently a company manages its assets and resource to generate sale and profit. By examining these ratios, entrepreneurs can identify areas of improvement, optimize their operation, and enhance their overall business performance. Financial ratios provide a valuable tool for entrepreneurs to communicate with potential investors, lenders, and stakeholder. These ratios offer a standardized model for presenting financial info and allow for easier comparing across company and industry. Investors and lenders often rely on financial ratios to assess a company's financial health and make informed investing decisions. By presenting strong financial ratios, entrepreneurs can instill trust in potential investors and improve their chance of securing financing for their business venture. Additionally, financial ratios can help entrepreneurs supervise and track their own business performance over clock. By regularly analyze and comparing ratios, entrepreneurs can identify trend, spot potential problem, and make timely adjustment to their business strategy. This ensures that their business remains on a solid financial foothold and continues to grow and thrive. Financial ratios serve as a powerful tool for performance benchmarking and competitive psychoanalysis. By comparing their ratios to industry peer or direct competitor, entrepreneurs can gain valuable insights into their business's relative strength and weakness. Understanding how their business measures up against competitor can help entrepreneurs identify areas for improvement, develop strategy for gaining a competitive vantage, and secure their marketplace stance. Financial ratios are essential for entrepreneurs in assessing their business performance and make informed financial decisions. These ratios provide critical insights into profitability, liquidity, solvency, and efficiency, enabling entrepreneurs to evaluate their financial health and identify areas of improvement. Financial ratios also facilitate communicating with investors and lenders, heighten business decision-making, and enable performance benchmarking.

By understanding and utilizing financial ratios effectively, entrepreneurs can effectively manage their money and grow their business.

TECHNIQUES FOR ANALYZING FINANCIAL RATIOS AND MAKING INFORMED DECISIONS BASED ON THE RESULTS

One of the most essential tool in financial analysis is the use of ratios. Ratios allow entrepreneurs to evaluate their business's financial health and make informed decisions based on the results. There are various techniques for analyzing financial ratios that entrepreneurs can employ to gain insights into different aspects of their business. One common technique is trend analysis, which involves comparing financial ratios over a point of clock to identify pattern and trend. By analyzing trend, entrepreneurs can determine whether their business's financial performance is improving or deteriorating and make necessary adjustment accordingly. It can also help entrepreneurs identify areas of their business that require care or improvement. Another technique is industry comparison, where entrepreneurs compare their financial ratios to those of other company in the same industry. This allows entrepreneurs to benchmark their business's financial performance against competitor and gain insights into areas where they may be underperforming or outperforming. By analyzing industry benchmark, entrepreneurs can get a better understanding of their business's competitive stance in the marketplace and make informed decisions to improve profitability and efficiency. Ratio analysis can also help entrepreneurs evaluate their business's liquidity, profitability, and solvency. Liquidity ratios, such as the current ratio and the quick ratio, measure a business's ability to meet its short-term obligations. By analyzing liquidity ratios, entrepreneurs can determine whether their business has enough liquid asset to cover its current liability, which is crucial for maintaining the day-to-day operation of the business. Profitability ratios, such as the gross profit leeway and the rejoin on fairness, measure a business's ability to generate profit from its operation. By analyzing profitability ratios, entrepreneurs can assess their business's profitability comparative to its sale, expense, and investing. Solvency ratios, such as the debt-to-equity ratio and the concern reportage ratio, measure a business's ability to meet its long-term obligations. By analyzing solvency ratios, entrepreneurs can evaluate their business's financial constancy and determine whether it is at danger of insolvency. In plus to these techniques, entrepreneurs should also consider the limitations and potential pitfalls associated with ratio analysis. It is important to ensure that the financial statement used for ratio analysis are accurate and reliable. Information error or inconsistency can distort the results and lead to incorrect conclusion. Entrepreneurs should also be mindful of the limitations of financial ratios as standalone measure of business performance. Ratios provide a snap of a business's financial health at a given level in clock, but they do not capture the full complexity and dynamic of a business. Entrepreneurs should use ratios in conjunction with other financial analysis techniques to obtain a comprehensive understanding of their business's financial performance and make informed decisions based on the results. The techniques for analyzing financial ratios are essential for entrepreneurs to evaluate their business's financial health and make informed decisions. These techniques include trend analysis, industry comparison, and valuation of liquidity, profitability, and solvency. By utilizing these techniques, entrepreneurs can gain insights into different aspects of their business and identify areas for improvement. Entrepreneurs should also be aware of the limitations and potential pitfalls associated with ratio analysis and use ratios in conjunction with other financial analysis techniques to obtain a comprehensive understanding of their business's financial performance. In the globe of entrepreneurship, understanding and effectively managing finances is crucial for the achiever and growth of a business. Financial management plays a pivotal part in the decision-making procedure, strategic plan, and overall performance of an entrepreneurial adventure. Properly managing finances allows entrepreneurs to allocate resources effectively, evaluate profitability, assess risks, and make informed decisions that align with business goal. By acquiring a solid understanding of fundamental financial principles and applying them to their business, entrepreneurs can navigate the complex financial landscape, ensure sustainable growth, and maximize to valuate of their initiative. One fundamental financial principle that entrepreneurs must grasp is budgeting. Budgeting involve creating a comprehensive program that outlines projected revenues, expense, and cash flow for the coming month or days. It provides entrepreneurs with a roadmap for financial decision-making and helps them determine whether their business operation are financially sustainable. By tracking and analyzing actual financial performance against the budget, entrepreneurs can identify area of chance or worry and adapt their strategy accordingly. Entrepreneurs also need to understand the concept of cash flow management. Cash flow refer to the drift of money into and out of a business and is crucial for its day-to-day operation. Monitoring cash flow allows entrepreneurs to ensure that there is enough money available to cover expense and meet financial obligation such as lend payment and payroll. By maintaining a positive cash flow, entrepreneurs can avoid liquid issue, minimize the need for external financing, and maintain financial constancy. Entrepreneurs should familiarize themselves with financial statement analysis. Financial statements, such as equilibrium sheet, income statements, and cash flow statements, provide crucial info about a business's financial stance and performance. Entrepreneurs must be able to interpret these statements to assess their party's profitability, liquid, solvency, and efficiency. Financial statement analysis enables entrepreneurs to identify strength and weakness within their business, make informed decisions, and establish benchmark for future financial performance. An understanding of risk management is also indispensable for entrepreneurs. Every business faces various risks, such as marketplace unpredictability, economic downturn, and change in client preference. Entrepreneurs need to identify these risks, assess their potential affect, and develop strategy to mitigate them. Risk management involves identifying, analyzing, and minimizing potential threat to a business's financial wellness and repute. By diversifying revenues, implementing risk management framework, and having eventuality plan in spot, entrepreneurs can protect their business against unforeseen event and secure its long-term viability. Additionally, entrepreneurs should be mindful of funding options and capital structure decisions. Raising capital is a critical facet of entrepreneurship, and entrepreneurs need to explore different funding sources, such as loan, fairness financing, or administration grant. By understanding the advantage and disadvantage of each financing option, entrepreneurs can make informed decisions on how to optimize their capital structure. Entrepreneurs must consider the price of capital and equilibrium it against expected return on investment to ensure optimal financial performance. Understanding the concept of evaluation is essential for entrepreneurs seeking to grow their business. Evaluation determines the monetary deserving of a business and is crucial for attracting investor, negotiating acquisition, or making strategic investment decisions. Entrepreneurs must understand evaluation methodology and factor that influence a business's valuate, such as revenue growth, profitability, marketplace dynamic, and intellectual belongings. By valuing their business accurately, entrepreneurs can negotiate favorable investment term and maximize their rejoin on investment. Understanding fundamental financial principles and applying them to their business is vital for entrepreneurs. Right financial management empower entrepreneurs to allocate resources effectively, evaluate profitability, assess risks, and make informed decisions that drive business growth. By incorporating budget, cash flow management, financial statement analysis, risk management, funding options, capital structure decisions, and evaluation into their financial scheme, entrepreneurs can navigate the complex financial landscape and achieve long-term achiever.

X. TAX PLANNING AND COMPLIANCE

Entrepreneurs must have a solid understanding of the tax implications associated with their business activities and ensure compliance with the relevant tax laws and regulations. Effective tax planning involves strategic decision-making to minimize tax liabilities while maximizing tax benefits. This requires entrepreneurs to be knowledgeable about the various tax incentive, deduction, and credit available to them. By taking advantage of this opportunity, entrepreneurs can lower their overall tax onus and improve their business cash flow. Additionally, entrepreneurs should also be aware of potential tax pitfall and ensure that they are in compliance with all tax laws and regulations. Nonstarter to do so can result in penalty, concern, and even legal issue. Regularly reviewing and updating tax compliance practice is essential to ensure that the business remains in good standing with the tax government. Tax planning should be an ongoing procedure that consider changes in tax laws, business operation, and the overall economic landscape. By staying informed about tax legislating and seeking professional advice when needed, entrepreneurs can adapt their tax strategy accordingly and stay ahead of any potential tax challenge. Entrepreneurs should maintain proper corroboration and record to support their tax position. This includes maintaining accurate financial record, receipt, and invoice, as well as documenting any expense or deduction claimed. A well-organized scheme for tax corroboration not only provides prove of tax compliance but also simplifies the tax file procedure and reduces the likeliness of error or audit. In addition to tax planning and compliance, entrepreneurs should also consider the tax implications associated with different business structure. Choosing the right legal entity, such as a sole proprietary, partnership, corp, or limited indebtedness party (LLC) , can have significant tax consequence. Each business construction has its own unique tax advantages and disadvantage, so it is essential for entrepreneurs to thoroughly understand these implications before making a determination. Consulting with a tax professional can help entrepreneurs navigate the complexity of tax planning for different business structure and make informed choice that align with their financial goal. Tax planning should not be approached in isolation but should be integrated into the overall financial management of the business. Entrepreneurs should develop a comprehensive financial plan that takes into calculate the affect of tax on their profitability, cash flow, and long-term financial objective. This includes budget for tax payment, estimating tax liabilities, and incorporating tax considerations into pricing strategy. By incorporating tax planning into their overall financial scheme, entrepreneurs can make more informed business decision and optimize their financial performance. Entrepreneurs should also be aware of the potential tax implications associated with international business activities. International taxation is an intricate and dynamic region that requires specialized cognition. Entrepreneurs who engage in cross-border transaction, such as import and exporting commodity or providing service to foreign customer, should be aware of the tax implications in different jurisdiction and seek professional advice to ensure compliance. Additionally, entrepreneurs should be aware of any tax treaty or agreement between country that may provide tax advantages or forestall double taxation. Having a solid understanding of international tax considerations is essential for entrepreneurs looking to expand their business globally and navigate the complex globe of international taxation. Tax planning and compliance are critical component of effective financial management for entrepreneurs. By understanding the tax implications of their business activities, seeking professional advice when necessary, and staying informed about changes in tax laws, entrepreneurs can minimize tax liabilities, maximize tax benefits, and ensure compliance with tax regulations. Incorporating tax planning into the overall financial management of the business allows entrepreneurs to make more informed decision, optimize their financial performance, and achieve long-term achiever.

TAX PLANNING FOR ENTREPRENEURS

Tax planning plays a key role in the effective management of your finances and ensures the growth and sustainability of your business. Entrepreneurs are individual who embark on a journeying of creating, developing, and managing their own businesses. As they navigate through various challenge and opportunity, tax planning becomes an essential element of their financial management scheme. By effectively planning their taxes, entrepreneurs can minimize their tax liability, maximize their deductions, and optimize their cash flow. One of the key benefit of tax planning is the decrease of tax liability. Entrepreneurs can achieve this by making informed decisions about the legal deductions and credit available to them. By taking vantage of tax incentives and exemption, entrepreneurs can significantly lower their overall tax burden. This decrease in taxes directly translates to increased profit and cash flow for their businesses. Additionally, tax planning enables entrepreneurs to leverage tax-efficient investing strategy such as utilizing retreat plan and tax-deferred account. By making strategic investment, entrepreneurs can not only minimize their current tax liability but also ensure future financial protection through long-term saving and investing increase. Tax planning empower entrepreneurs to make informed decisions about their business structure and entity type. Choosing the right business structure, whether it be a sole proprietary, partnership, corp, or limited liability party (LLC) , can have significant significance on the taxes entrepreneurs are required to pay. Through careful tax planning, entrepreneurs can evaluate the professional and con of each entity type and select the single that aligns with their business goal and tax objective. This allows entrepreneurs to minimize their self-employment taxes, maximize their deductions, and optimize their overall tax stance. Tax planning also enables entrepreneurs to effectively manage their cash flow. By understanding the nuance of tax laws and regulations, entrepreneurs can anticipate their tax liability and plan for them accordingly. This involves projecting their expected income, expense, and deductions to estimate their tax liability for the upcoming year. By doing so, entrepreneurs can allocate fund for tax payment systematically, avoiding any sudden financial burden or cash shortage. This proactive overture to tax planning ensures that entrepreneurs have sufficient liquid to meet their tax obligation and sustain their businesses' operation smoothly. Additionally, tax planning facilitate effective financial decision-making for entrepreneurs. By evaluating the tax significance of various business activity and transaction, entrepreneurs can make informed choice that maximize after-tax benefit. Tax planning can help entrepreneurs assess the tax consequence of purchasing new equipment or asset for their businesses. By considering factor such as derogation, uppercase allowance, and other tax incentives, entrepreneurs can determine the optimal time and funding strategy for their investment. Tax planning also plays a significant role in mitigating potential tax risk and ensuring compliance with tax laws and regulations. By staying updated on the latest tax laws, entrepreneurs can identify potential area of exposure and implement measure to minimize their tax vulnerability. Through effective tax planning, entrepreneurs can prevent any legal or financial repercussion arising from non-compliance or ignorance of tax regulations. Tax planning is a crucial facet of financial management for entrepreneurs. By strategically managing their taxes, entrepreneurs can reduce their tax burden, optimize their cash flow, and make informed financial decisions. Tax planning enables entrepreneurs to select the appropriate business structure, plan for their tax liability, and navigate the complexity of tax laws and regulations. For entrepreneurs looking to grow their businesses and achieve long-term financial achiever, tax planning is an indispensable instrument that must be utilized effectively.

STRATEGIES FOR MINIMIZING TAX LIABILITIES LEGALLY

There are several strategies that entrepreneurs can employ to achieve this aim. Firstly, they can take advantage of available tax deductions and credits. By carefully tracking their business expense, entrepreneurs can identify deductions that they are eligible for, such as post lease, utility, employee salary, and ad cost. Additionally, they can also explore credits that they qualify for, such as the inquiry and developing Tax Credit or the minuscule Business wellness Care Tax Credit. By maximizing these deductions and credits, entrepreneurs can significantly reduce their taxable income, thereby minimizing their tax liabilities. Secondly, entrepreneurs can construction their business entities in a way that provides tax advantages. For instance, they can consider forming a limited indebtedness party (LLC) or an S corp, as these entities offer certain tax benefit. A single-member LLC can be treated as a disregarded entity for tax purpose, meaning that the proprietor's income is reported on their personal tax rejoin. This allows for simplified tax reportage and potentially lower tax rate. Similarly, an S corp can provide tax advantages by allowing the business income to pass through to the shareholder' personal tax return, avoiding double tax. By carefully choosing the appropriate business entity, entrepreneurs can optimize their tax situation and minimize their tax liabilities. Thirdly, entrepreneurs can take advantage of tax-deferred or tax-free investment options. For instance, they can contribute to retreat plan such as private retreat account (IRA) or Simplified Employee Pension (Sept) IRA. This contribution are tax-deductible and can help reduce taxable income. By investing in tax-advantaged retreat account, entrepreneurs can benefit from tax-deferred growth and potentially lower their tax liabilities in the long-running. Entrepreneurs can also explore tax-free investment such as municipal bond, which provide income that is exempt from federal tax and sometimes commonwealth and local tax. By strategically incorporating these investment options into their financial planning, entrepreneurs can minimize their tax liabilities legally while simultaneously building riches for their next. Entrepreneurs can utilize tax planning strategies to minimize their tax liabilities. This involves proactively organizing their finances to take advantage of favorable tax law and regulation. For instance, they can clock income and expense in a way that optimizes their tax situation. By deferring income to a later year or accelerating deductions into the current year, entrepreneurs can potentially lower their taxable income and reduce their overall tax liabilities. Additionally, they can implement tax-loss harvest strategies, which involve selling investment that have declined in valuate to offset gain in other investment. This can result in uppercase loss that can be used to offset uppercase gain, thereby reducing the tax consequence. By engaging in effective tax planning, entrepreneurs can actively manage their tax liabilities and minimize their tax burden within the boundary of the jurisprudence. Minimizing tax liabilities is a crucial facet of financial direction for entrepreneurs. By employing various strategies, entrepreneurs can legally reduce their tax liabilities and enhance their financial well-being. These strategies include taking advantage of tax deductions and credits, structuring business entities for tax advantages, utilizing tax-deferred or tax-free investment options, and implementing tax planning strategies. By carefully implementing these strategies, entrepreneurs can optimize their tax situation and allocate more resource towards growing their business and achieving long-term achiever.

COMPLYING WITH TAX REGULATIONS TO AVOID PENALTIES AND LEGAL ISSUES

The consequences of non-compliance can have severe significance for both the individual entrepreneur and their business. Firstly, complying with tax regulations ensures that entrepreneurs remain on the right side of the law, preventing potential legal issues that may arise. Tax law are complex and constantly evolving, making it imperative for entrepreneurs to stay up-to-date on the latest regulations to avoid any unintentional violation. By doing so, entrepreneurs can safeguard themselves from costly legal battles and potential harm to their professional reputation. Complying with tax regulations helps entrepreneurs avoid penalties and other financial consequences. Tax government have the force to impose several penalties for non-compliance, such as fines, interest charges, and even criminal charges in extreme case. These penalties can have a significant financial effect on both the entrepreneur and their business. For instance, hefty fines can eat into profit and cash flowing, hindering the growth and sustainability of the business. Additionally, interest charges can accumulate over clock, further exacerbating the financial onus. By complying with tax regulations, entrepreneurs can prevent these penalties, ensuring that their financial resource are allocated towards business growth instead of legal expense. Tax compliance is essential for construction and maintaining trust with investor, partners, and customers. Compliance demonstrates an entrepreneur's dedication to conducting business ethically and transparently. Investor are more likely to invest in a business that is in good stand with tax government, as it signals a lower tier of danger. Similarly, partners and customers prefer to engage with business that have a reputation for compliance, as it instills trust and trust in the party's financial practice. By adhering to tax regulations, entrepreneurs can cultivate a positive brand mark picture and attract valuable stakeholders, contributing to the growth and achiever of their business. Additionally, tax compliance foster a stable business environment and contribute to the overall economy. Tax collected by the administration are essential for funding public services and infrastructure, such as healthcare, teaching, and transport. By diligently fulfilling their tax obligation, entrepreneurs contribute to the sustainable developing and well-being of society as a whole. In counterpoint, non-compliance deprives the economy of vital tax revenue, potentially leading to resource shortage and limited administration expenditure. The resulting economic unbalance can negatively impact entrepreneurs and their business in the long-running. Ensuring tax compliance is not only a legal and financial duty for entrepreneurs, but also a civic obligation to support the broader community. Complying with tax regulations is of overriding grandness for entrepreneurs to avoid penalties and legal issues. By remaining on the right side of the law, entrepreneurs can protect themselves from costly legal battles and safeguard their professional reputation. Tax compliance prevent potential financial consequences, such as fines and interest charges, that can hinder the growth and sustainability of the business. Compliance also helps entrepreneurs build trust with stakeholders, contributing to their long-term achiever. Tax compliance plays a vital part in fostering a stable business environment and supporting the overall economy by ensuring the accessibility of public services and infrastructure. Through tax compliance, entrepreneurs can not only maintain their own financial unity but also contribute to the successfulness of their business and society as a whole. In now's competitive business surroundings, it is crucial for entrepreneurs to not only have innovative ideas but also possess a solid understanding of financial management principle in ordering to effectively grow their businesses. Financial management is a crucial facet of entrepreneurship as it involves making strategic decisions about the allotment of resource, managing cash flow, and evaluating the profitability of investment. Firstly, entrepreneurs need to have a clear understanding of financial statements and how they can be used to analyze the financial health of their businesses. Financial statements such as the income statement, equilibrium shroud, and cash flow statement provide vital info about the revenue, expenses, asset, liability, and cash flow of a business. By analyzing these statements, entrepreneurs can identify area of betterment, evaluate the profitability of their operation, and make informed decisions about resourcefulness allotment. Entrepreneurs need to be able to effectively manage their cash flow, which refers to the inflow and outflow of cash within a business. Cash flow management is crucial for the day-to-day operation of a business as it ensures that there is enough cash available to pay for expenses, salary, and other financial obligation. Implementing strategy such as managing account receivable and payable, negotiating favorable payment term with supplier, and closely monitoring cash flow projection can help entrepreneurs maintain positive cash flow and avoid financial difficulty. Entrepreneurs need to understand the conception of profitability and how it relates to their business operation. Profitability refers to the ability of a business to generate profits or profit over a point of clock. Entrepreneurs need to evaluate the profitability of their product or service, consider the cost involved in producing them, and determine whether they can be priced competitively in the marketplace. Calculating key financial ratio such as gross profit margin, net profit margin, and return on investing can help entrepreneurs assess the profitability of their business and make informed decisions about price, price decrease, and enlargement strategy. Additionally, entrepreneurs need to have a comprehensive understanding of the different source of financing available to them and how to raise capital for their business. Financing is essential for entrepreneurs to start and grow their businesses, and they need to explore various option such as personal saving, kinfolk and friend, deposit loan, adventure capital, and crowdfunding. Each generator of financing has its own advantage and disadvantage, and entrepreneurs need to carefully evaluate these option and select the one that align with their business objective, danger permissiveness, and financial capability. Alongside raising capital, entrepreneurs also need to be able to effectively manage their personal finances and separate them from their business finances. Separating personal and business finances is crucial for maintaining accurate financial record, ensuring taxation compliance, and protecting personal asset. Entrepreneurs should establish separate deposit account, recognition card, and financial statements for their businesses and themselves. This clear breakup will not only help entrepreneurs manage their finances more effectively but also provide a clear photograph of the financial health of their business, making it easier to secure financing or attract investor. The effective management of finances is crucial for the achiever of entrepreneurs and their businesses. By understanding financial statements, managing cash flow, evaluating profitability, raising capital, and separating personal and business finances, entrepreneurs can make informed decisions and grow their businesses sustainably. Financial management is a fundamental accomplishment that every entrepreneur should possess as it enables them to navigate the complex financial landscape and turn their innovative ideas into profitable venture.

XI. FINANCIAL CONTROLS AND INTERNAL AUDIT

The aim of financial controls is to ensure the accuracy and dependability of financial information, as well as to promote compliance with law and regulation. Internal audit plays a crucial role in the implementation and valuation of financial controls. Internal audit is an independent, objective confidence, and consulting activeness designed to add valuate to an organization. It helps business accomplish their objective by bringing a systematic, disciplined overture to evaluate and improve the effectiveness of risk management, control, and governance processes. Internal auditors ensure that financial controls are properly designed, implemented, and operating effectively. One of the key component of financial controls is the segregation of duties. This precept ensures that no single employee has control over all aspect of a financial transaction. By separating authorizing, recording, and detention function, business can minimize the risk of errors, fraud, and embezzlement of assets. The internal audit operate evaluates the segregation of duties within an organization to ensure that financial transactions are adequately safeguarded. Another important aspect of financial controls is the establishment of proper authorization processes. This involves providing appropriate level of authorization to employee for making financial decision and executing transactions. Internal auditors play a crucial role in assessing whether the authorization processes are well-defined, communicated, and consistently followed throughout the organization. Financial control also involves regular monitoring and oversight of financial transactions. This can be achieved through the implementation of reexamination processes and the utilize of key execution indicator (KPIs) to bill and monitor the financial execution of the business. Internal auditors evaluate the effectiveness of the monitoring and oversight processes to ensure that they are sufficient to detect and prevent errors, fraud, and non-compliance. Effective financial controls also require the implementation of physical safeguards and security measure. This includes the establishment of secure physical environment, such as locked filing cabinet or restricted admittance area, to protect sensitive financial information and assets. Internal auditors verify the adequacy and effectiveness of these physical safeguards to mitigate the risk of unauthorized admittance and larceny. Financial controls should include the implementation of automated controls and information systems to enhance the efficiency and accuracy of financial processes. Internal auditors assess the designing, implementation, and procedure of these automated controls and information systems to ensure that they are reliable and effectively support financial controls. An important aspect of financial control is the establishment of policies and procedure that guide the financial activity of the business. Internal auditors evaluate the adequacy, completeness, and accuracy of these policies and procedure to ensure that they are effectively communicated, understand, and consistently followed throughout the organization. Financial controls and internal audit play a critical role in managing the financial wellness of a business. By implementing and evaluating the effectiveness of financial controls, entrepreneurs can minimize the risk of financial errors, fraud, and non-compliance. Internal auditors provide independent confidence and consulting service to help business achieve their financial objective and improve their risk management, control, and governance processes. Through the implementation of segregation of duties, proper authorization processes, monitoring and oversight, physical safeguards and security measure, automated controls and information systems, and well-defined policies and procedure, entrepreneurs can establish a strong financial foundation and ensure the accuracy, dependability, and compliance of their financial information.

DEFINITION AND SIGNIFICANCE OF FINANCIAL CONTROLS

Financial controls cite to the system, procedures, and policy that organization put in spot to ensure the efficient and effective management of their financial resources. These controls play a crucial part in the success and sustainability of businesses. Financial controls encompass a wide range of activities, including budgeting, internal audits, risk management, and financial reporting, among others. The primary aim of financial controls is to mitigate risks, ensure compliance with laws and regulations, and safeguard assets. By implementing robust financial controls, organization can not only minimize the likelihood of fraudulence, errors, and embezzlement of fund but also establish a solid foundation for making informed decisions and achieving their financial goals. One fundamental aspect of financial controls is budgeting. A budget serves as a roadmap for businesses, helping them to plan their financial activities, allocate resources efficiently, and evaluate their execution. It allows entrepreneurs to set realistic goals, monitor their progression, and make adjustment if necessary. A well-designed budget takes into calculate both the income and expenses of a business, ensuring that expenditure are in pipeline with available resources. By adhering to a budget, entrepreneurs can gain insight into their business's cash flowing, identify areas of excessive expenditure or possible price saving, and make informed financial decisions. Internal audits are another critical aspect of financial controls. Internal audits are systematic and independent exam of a party's financial and operational activities conducted by internal auditor.

These audits provide an objective valuation of how well an establishment is adhering to its policy and procedures, identify potential weakness or areas of betterment, and assess the potency of risk management strategy. Internal audits help entrepreneurs to identify and address any inefficiency, errors, or fraudulent activities that may be occurring within their establishment. By regularly conducting internal audits, businesses can enhance their internal controls and mitigate potential risks, ensuring the integrity and reliability of their financial information. Risk management is an integral component of financial controls. Businesses face a wide range of risks, including financial, operational, legal, and reputational risks. Effective risk management involves identifying, assessing, and mitigating these risks to protect the establishment's assets, repute, and financial well-being. Financial controls help entrepreneurs to implement risk management strategy through mechanism such as separatism of duty, authority controls, and internal control system. These controls provide a model for ensuring that decisions are made based on precise and reliable information, reducing the likelihood of errors and fraudulence. By proactively managing risks, businesses can minimize potential loss and seize opportunity that may arise. Financial reporting is another critical element of financial controls. Timely and accurate financial reporting allows entrepreneurs to track the financial execution of their business and communicate it to stakeholder, such as investor, lender, and regulatory body. Financial reporting provides a comprehensive photograph of a business's financial stance, including its assets, liability, revenue, and expenses. It enables entrepreneurs to assess the profitability and solvency of their business, make strategic decisions, and follow with legal and regulatory requirement. Financial controls ensure that financial reporting is prepared in conformity with generally accepted accountancy principle, thus enhancing the transparency and believability of the information provided. Financial controls are essential for the success and sustainability of businesses. These controls encompass a wide range of activities, including budgeting, internal audits, risk management, and financial reporting. By implementing robust financial controls, entrepreneurs can mitigate risks, ensure compliance with laws and regulations, and safeguard assets. Financial controls provide a solid foundation for making informed decisions, plan and allocating resources efficiently, and achieving financial goals. Additionally, financial controls enhance the integrity and reliability of financial information, strengthen the internal control surroundings, and foster transparency and answerability within organization. Entrepreneurs must prioritize the formation and upkeep of effective financial controls to manage their money and grow their businesses.

TECHNIQUES FOR IMPLEMENTING EFFECTIVE FINANCIAL CONTROLS IN A BUSINESS

These controls are necessary to ensure that a business is operating efficiently and that its financial resources are being managed effectively. There are several techniques that entrepreneurs can employ to implement these controls and ensure the financial constancy of their business. The first technique is creating a budget. A budget is a financial program that outlines the expected revenue and expense of a business over a specific point of clock. By creating a budget, entrepreneurs can set financial goals and track their progression towards achieving them. This allows them to make informed decisions about how to allocate resources and identify area where cost can be reduced or receipts can be increased. Another technique for implementing effective financial controls is establishing financial policies and procedures. These policies and procedures provide guideline for how financial transactions should be handled within the business. They outline who has authorization to make financial decisions, how financial record should be maintained, and what financial reporting requirement must be met. By establishing clear policies and procedures, entrepreneurs can ensure that financial transactions are conducted in a consistent and accurate way. This helps to prevent error and fraudulence and ensures that financial info is reliable and meaningful. A third technique for implementing effective financial controls is regularly monitoring and analyzing financial performance. This involves reviewing financial report and comparing them to established goals and benchmark. By regularly monitoring financial performance, entrepreneurs can quickly identify any deviation from the program and take corrective action. This may involve adjusting the budget, reallocating resources, or implementing cost-saving measure. In plus to monitoring financial performance, entrepreneurs should also conduct periodic financial analyses to gain insight into the financial wellness of their business. This may involve calculating financial ratios, such as liquid ratios, profitability ratios, and efficiency ratios, to assess the business's power to meet its short-term and long-term obligation, engender profit, and utilize its resources effectively. A fourth technique for implementing effective financial controls is implementing internal controls. Internal controls are the processes and procedures that a business puts in spot to safeguard its asset, ensure the truth of its financial record, and promote operational efficiency. Example of internal controls include separatism of duty, requiring approving for financial transactions, conducting periodic physical count of inventorying, and regularly reconciling deposit statement with the business's financial record. By implementing internal controls, entrepreneurs can mitigate the danger of error, fraudulence, and misdirection, and ensure that their business's financial resources are protected. Entrepreneurs can implement effective financial controls by regularly reviewing and updating their business's financial systems and processes. As technology and business practice evolve, it is important for entrepreneurs to periodically assess their financial systems and processes to ensure that they remain effective and efficient. This may involve upgrading accountancy package, implementing new financial reporting tool, or streamlining financial processes to reduce cost and improve truth. By regularly reviewing and updating their financial systems and processes, entrepreneurs can capitalize on opportunity for betterment and ensure that their business's financial controls remain effective in to confront of changing circumstance. Implementing effective financial controls is crucial for the achiever of any business. By creating a budget, establishing financial policies and procedures, monitoring and analyzing financial performance, implementing internal controls, and regularly reviewing and updating financial systems and processes, entrepreneurs can ensure that their business is operating efficiently, and their financial resources are being managed effectively. By employing this technique, entrepreneurs can make informed financial decisions, palliate risk, and stance their business for long-term achiever.

THE ROLE OF INTERNAL AUDIT IN ENSURING FINANCIAL TRANSPARENCY AND ACCOUNTABILITY

They act as a mechanics to assess and evaluate the effectiveness of an organization's internal controls, risk management processes, and compliance with relevant laws and regulations. By conducting regular and independent review of financial data and processes, internal auditors help identify any discrepancy or irregularities that may exist within an organization's financial statements or operation. The primary aim of an internal audit is to provide reasonable assurance on the reliability and unity of an organization's financial reportage. Internal auditors achieve this aim by assessing the effectiveness of internal controls that govern the organization's financial activity. By examining the designing and execution of control system, internal auditors can identify weakness or gap that may expose the organization to financial risks or fraudulence. Through the valuation of control processes, such as separatism of duty, approving government, and corroboration procedures, internal auditors can ensure that financial transaction are accurately recorded, authorized, and reported. Financial transparency is another vital facet that internal auditors help to achieve. Transparency refers to the availability and clearness of an organization's financial information for stakeholders, including shareholder, investor, and regulatory government. Internal auditors play a pivotal role in ensuring that financial statements provide a true and fair perspective of an

organization's financial stance by scrutinizing critical accountancy estimate, revelation practices, and adhesion to accountancy principle. By reviewing financial reports and disclosure, internal auditors can identify any misstatement or omission that
may compromise the transparency of financial information. This
helps in ensuring that stakeholders have reliable and accurate
financial data to make informed decisions about the organization. Internal auditors also contribute to enhancing accountability within organizations. Accountability refers to the duty and
obligation of individual or entity to be answerable for their actions or decisions. Internal auditors help hold individual ac-
countable by objectively assessing their compliance with policy,
procedures, and the relevant laws and regulations. Through the
reexamination and exam of financial activity, internal auditors
can detect any non-compliant behavior, financial irregularities,
or unethical practices. By reporting such finding to management
and the panel of director, internal auditors play a significant role
in ensuring that individual are held responsible for their actions
and decisions and that appropriate actions are taken to rectify
any identified deficiency. Additionally, the role of internal audits
in ensuring financial transparency and accountability extends
beyond the financial statements. Internal auditors are increasingly involved in evaluating an organization's overall risk management processes. By assessing the effectiveness of an organization's risk recognition, appraisal, and extenuation strategy,
internal auditors help ensure that potential financial risks are
identified and managed appropriately. This includes risks related to fraudulence, wastage, inadequate controls, or non-
compliance with laws and regulations. Through their assessment, internal auditors help organizations improve their risk

management practices, thereby enhancing transparency and accountability. Internal audits play a significant role in ensuring financial transparency and accountability within organizations. Through the appraisal of internal controls, compliance with laws and regulations, and the reliability of financial statements, internal auditors help identify any weakness, irregularities, or non-compliant behavior. Their objective valuation provides reasonable assurance about the truth and reliability of financial information for stakeholders. Internal auditors also contribute to enhancing accountability by holding individual responsible for their actions and decisions and assisting in risk management evaluation. The role of internal audits is critical in fostering confidence in an organization's financial reports and promoting sound financial management practices. In ordering for entrepreneurs to successfully manage their finances and grow their businesses, it is crucial for them to understand the fundamental financial principles and know how to apply them effectively. One such principle is the concept of budget. Budgeting involves the estimate and allotment of finances to different aspect of a business, such as merchandising, operation, and inquiry and developing. By creating a budget, entrepreneurs are able to plan and monitor their expenses, ensuring that they are in pipeline with their receipts and overall business goals. This allows them to make informed decisions and avoid overspend or running into financial difficulty. Another important financial principle is cash flow direction. Cash flow refers to the drift of money in and out of a business, and managing it effectively is essential for the long-term success of any entrepreneurial adventure. By monitoring cash inflow and outflow on a regular fundament, entrepreneurs can ensure that they have enough liquid to cover their expenses and meet their financial obligation. This includes paying supplier, employee, and lender on clock, as well as maintaining an adequate level of working uppercase to support day-to-day operation. Effective cash flow direction also involves having a clear understand of the time of cash flow, such as when customer is likely to make payment and when expenses are due, allowing entrepreneurs to plan and prepare accordingly. A key financial principle for entrepreneurs to grasp is the concept of financial leverage. Financial leverage refers to utilize of borrowed fund to finance business operation or investment. While it can be a useful instrument for entrepreneurs, as it allows them to leverage their own uppercase and potentially generate higher return, it also carries certain risks. High level of leverage can lead to higher concern expenses and potentially increase the business's financial exposure. Entrepreneurs need to carefully evaluate the potential benefit and risks associated with using leverage and determine the appropriate level of debt to take on based on their business's financial shape and risk permissiveness. Additionally, entrepreneurs need to understand the grandness of financial forecasting and planning. Financial forecasting involve estimating future financial outcome based on historical information and current trend. By conducting financial forecasts, entrepreneurs can identify potential opportunity and risks, make informed business decisions, and set realistic financial goals. It also facilitates the developing of a comprehensive financial plan that outlines the strategy and action needed to achieve those goals. This includes determining the appropriate mixture of debt and fairness funding, setting price strategy, and allocating resource effectively. By regularly review and updating their financial forecasts and plan, entrepreneurs can adapt to changing marketplace weather and make necessary adjustment to ensure their business's financial increase and sustainability. The effective direction of finances is crucial for entrepreneurs in ordering to grow their businesses. By understanding and applying fundamental financial principles, such as budget, cash flow direction, financial leverage, and financial forecasting and planning, entrepreneurs can make informed decisions that lead to long-term success. These principles allow entrepreneurs to allocate their resource efficiently, maintain a healthy cash flow, leverage their uppercase effectively, and set realistic financial goals. By applying these financial principles, entrepreneurs can effectively manage their money and grow their businesses.

XII. FINANCIAL MANAGEMENT SOFTWARE AND TOOLS

These tools provide valuable insights and aid in managing and growing a business's finance effectively. One popular financial management software is QuickBooks, which offers an array of feature designed to simplify financial tasks and improve overall efficiency. With QuickBooks, entrepreneurs can easily track their income and expenses, generate financial report, and even handle payroll management. Another widely used tool is Fresh-Books, an accountancy software specifically tailored for small business and freelance. FreshBooks allows entrepreneurs to track their clock, create professional invoice, and communicate effectively with client, all in one user-friendly program. In addition to this software solution, there are various other financial management tools that entrepreneurs can leverage to improve their financial decision-making processes. Budget tools, such as coin, and You Need a Budget (NAB) , assist entrepreneurs in creating and sticking to budget by providing real-time update on income and expenses. These tools also offer insights into expenditure patterns, allowing entrepreneurs to identify area where they can cut cost and save money. Financial forecasting tools like Plan Guru and Projection Hub enable entrepreneurs to project future revenue and expenses and make informed financial decision based on this projection. By utilizing these tools, entrepreneurs can better anticipate cash flow fluctuation and take appropriate measure to mitigate financial risk. Financial management software and tools enable entrepreneurs to monitor and manage their business's financial health more effectively. Cash flow management tools, such as pulsing and swim, provide entrepreneurs with real-time insights into their cash flow stance, allowing them to identify potential cash shortage or surplus and take necessary action accordingly. Similarly, debtor management tools like Zoho bill and Invoice Sherpa simplify the process of tracking and collecting payment from customer, thereby improving the overall cash flow of the business. With the assist of these tools, entrepreneurs can streamline their cash flow management processes and minimize the danger of cash flow disruption. Financial management software and tools offer entrepreneurs enhanced profile into their business's financial execution. Analytics and reportage tools, such as Tableau and Microsoft ability bismuth, allow entrepreneurs to collect, examine, and visualize financial information in a meaningful path. These tools enable entrepreneurs to gain valuable insights into key execution indicator, such as receipts increase, profitability, and return on investing, which can guide their decision-making processes. Additionally, these tools can help entrepreneurs identify trend, patterns, and potential area for betterment within their business operation. By leveraging these insights, entrepreneurs can make data-driven decision that support their financial goal and driving business increase. To sum up, financial management software and tools are essential resource for entrepreneurs seeking to manage their money effectively and grow their business. These tools simplify various financial tasks, such as budget, cash flow management, and financial forecasting, allowing entrepreneurs to focus on nucleus business activity. Additionally, these tools provide entrepreneurs with valuable insights into their business's financial health and execution, enabling them to make informed decision and take appropriate action. As the business surroundings continues to evolve, it is crucial for entrepreneurs to embrace this technological advancement and leverage them to their vantage. By doing so, entrepreneurs can navigate the complex financial landscape with alleviate and maximize their business's increase possible.

FINANCIAL MANAGEMENT SOFTWARE AND TOOLS AVAILABLE TO ENTREPRENEURS

In now's modern business landscape, there is a wide range of software applications and tools available to entrepreneurs that can simplify and streamline financial management process. One popular alternative is accounting software, which helps entrepreneurs disc and track their company's financial transaction, generate financial statements, and manage day-to-day accounting tasks. Examples of widely used accounting software include QuickBooks, Hero, and FreshBooks. These software applications are user-friendly, affordable, and provide entrepreneurs with real-time insights into their company's financial health. Another important tool available to entrepreneurs is budgeting and forecasting software. These tools enable entrepreneurs to create a comprehensive budget, set financial goals, and generate forecast and projection based on various scenarios. By using budgeting and forecasting software, entrepreneurs can make informed financial decisions, plan for growth, and identify potential issue or risk. Some popular budgeting and forecasting tools include Adaptive Insights, Profit, and Plan Guru. Additionally, financial analytics software is becoming increasingly popular among entrepreneurs as it provides valuable insights into the company's financial information. Financial analytics software allows entrepreneurs to analyze key financial metric, identify trend, and make data-driven decisions. Examples of financial analytics tools include Tableau, ability bismuth, and Olivier. These tools help entrepreneurs gain a deeper understanding of their business's financial performance, profitability, and cash flowing, enabling them to make well-informed decisions and drive growth. In plus to specific software applications, there are also various online platforms and services that provide a comprehensive suite of financial management tools for entrepreneurs. Roll offers a range of financial tools, including accounting, invoice, and payment process, all in one integrated platform. Coin is a popular personal finance app that entrepreneurs can use to track their personal and business expense, set budget, and monitor their financial goals. These platforms provide entrepreneurs with a centralized hub for managing their finances, streamlining tasks, and staying organized. Financial management software and tools can greatly benefit entrepreneurs by providing them with the necessary tools and insights to effectively manage their finances. These tools can help entrepreneurs save clock, reduce error, and gain a clear understanding of their company's financial health. By utilizing accounting software, entrepreneurs can automate clerking tasks and generate precise and up-to-date financial statements. Budgeting and forecasting tools allow entrepreneurs to plan for growth, identify potential risk, and make informed financial decisions. Financial analytics software provides entrepreneurs with valuable insights into the company's financial performance, enabling them to optimize their business operation and drive growth. Online platforms and services offer a comprehensive suite of financial management tools that entrepreneurs can leverage to streamline tasks and stay organized. The accessibility of financial management software and tools has revolutionized the path entrepreneurs handle their finances, empowering them to make informed financial decisions and successfully grow their businesses.

BENEFITS OF USING TECHNOLOGY FOR FINANCIAL MANAGEMENT

The benefits of using technology for financial management are numerous and can greatly facilitate the process of managing finances for entrepreneurs. One major benefit is the ability to quickly and efficiently track and analyze financial data. With the use of software and online tools, entrepreneurs can easily input and store financial information, such as income, expense, and cash flow. This allows them to have a real-time perspective of their financial position and make informed decisions regarding budget and financial planning. Additionally, technology can provide entrepreneurs with access to a wide range of financial resource and information. Through the use of mobile apps and online platforms, entrepreneurs can access financial tidings, marketplace trends, and investment opportunities, allowing them to stay up-to-date and make well-informed financial decisions. Another benefit of using technology for financial management is the automation of repetitive tasks. Many financial management tools offer features that automate tasks such as account generation, disbursement track, and financial reportage. This not only saves entrepreneurs time but also reduces the risk of human mistake in financial calculation. Technology can enhance collaboration and communicating in financial management. With the use of cloud-based software and platforms, entrepreneurs can deal financial data and cooperate with their squad member or financial advisor in real-time. This enables effective collaboration, improves transparency, and ensures that everyone involved is on the same foliate regarding the party's financial goals and progression. Technology can also provide entrepreneurs with improved truth and efficiency in financial forecast and planning. Financial management software can generate detailed financial report, projection, and forecast based on historical data and various assumptions. This can help entrepreneurs identify potential financial risk and opportunities, develop realistic financial goals, and make informed decisions regarding cash flow management, budget allotment, and investment strategy. Additionally, the use of technology can help entrepreneurs streamline financial process and reduce cost. By implementing online payment system and automated account process, entrepreneurs can save time and reduce the cost associated with manual payment process and paper-based invoice. Technology can help entrepreneurs gain valuable insights and make data-driven financial decisions. By leveraging data analytics tools, entrepreneurs can analyze financial pattern, trends, and metric, and gain a deeper understand of their financial execution. This can help them identify area for betterment, optimize receipts generation, and make strategic financial decisions that adjust with their clientele goals. The use of technology for financial management can enhance protection and reduce the risk of fraudulence. Many financial management tools offer advanced protection feature, such as encoding, two-factor certification, and regular data backup, to protect sensitive financial information from unauthorized access or cyberattacks. Additionally, technology can provide entrepreneurs with access to real-time monitor tools that can detect and alert them to any suspicious financial activity. The benefits of using technology for financial management are numerous and can greatly facilitate the process of managing finances for entrepreneurs. From the ability to track and analyze financial data in real-time to the automation of repetitive tasks and the proviso of valuable insights, technology offer entrepreneurs a range of tools and resource to effectively manage their finances, make informed decisions, and grow their business. By harnessing the force of technology, entrepreneurs can gain a competitive boundary in the increasingly digital and complex financial landscape.

FACTORS TO CONSIDER WHEN CHOOSING THE MOST SUITABLE SOFTWARE OR TOOL FOR A BUSINESS

Firstly, it is crucial to evaluate the specific needs and requirement of the business. This involves identifying the task and processes that the software or tool needs to handle. For instance, if the business requires accounting software, it is important to determine whether it needs basic clerking functionality or more advanced feature such as payroll direction and inventorying track. Understanding the specific needs of the business will help in narrowing down the option and selecting a software or tool that aligns with this requirement. Secondly, the scalability of the software or tool should be considered. As a business grow, its needs and demand also increase. It is essential to choose a software or tool that can accommodate the future increase of the business. This means ensuring that the software or tool has the capacity to handle a larger intensity of transaction, user, or information. Scalability is particularly important for startup and small businesses that anticipate rapid enlargement. Investing in a scalable software or tool can save the business from the fuss and disbursement of switching to a new system in the future. Another important factor to consider is compatibility with existing systems and processes. Businesses often have existing software, tool, or processes in spot that they rely on for their operations. When choosing a new software or tool, it is crucial to ensure that it can integrate smoothly with these existing systems. This may involve checking whether the software offers

APIs or other integrating option. Choosing a software or tool that is compatible with existing systems can save clock and attempt in the execution process and minimize interruption to the business's operations. Serviceability is also a critical factor to consider. The software or tool should be user-friendly and easy to navigate. It should have a clear and intuitive port that requires minimal preparation or supporting. This is particularly important for businesses that do not have dedicated IT faculty or extensive technical expertness. A user-friendly software or tool can help ensure a smoother changeover and minimize the learn bend for employee. Price is another key circumstance. Businesses need to evaluate the price of acquiring and maintaining the software or tool. This includes not only the upfront price but also any ongoing fee, such as license or subscription fee. It is important to determine whether the software or tool provides valuate for money and whether the benefit outweighs the cost. Additionally, it is worth considering whether there are any hidden cost, such as execution or customization expense. Conducting a cost-benefit psychoanalysis can help businesses make an informed decision and avoid any unexpected financial burden. It is advisable to seek recommendation and review from other businesses or manufacture expert. This can provide valuable insight and help in assessing the suitability and dependability of the software or tool. Online forum, social medium group, and manufacture conference are all good source for gathering feedback and opinion. Taking the clock to inquiry and gathering info can help in making an informed decision and selecting a software or tool that has a proven racetrack disc. When choosing the most suitable software or tool for a business, it is important to consider factor such as specific needs, scalability, compatibility, serviceability, price, and recommendation. Evaluating these factor will help businesses make an informed decision and select a software or tool that aligns with their requirement and contribute to their achiever. The foundation of every successful business is solid financial management. It is crucial for entrepreneurs to understand fundamental financial principle and apply them to their business in ordering to achieve sustainable growth. One of the key aspect of financial management is budgeting. A budget serves as a roadmap for the allotment and usage of financial resource. By creating a budget, entrepreneurs can plan and control their expense, identify areas of potential price saving, and make informed decisions about resourcefulness allotment. Additionally, budgeting allow entrepreneurs to set financial goal and monitor their progression towards achieving them. By regularly reviewing their budget and comparing it to actual figure, entrepreneurs can identify any discrepancy and take corrective action if necessary. Another important aspect of financial management is cash flow management. Cash flow refer to the drift of money in and out of a business. It is essential for entrepreneurs to closely monitor their cash flow to ensure that they have enough liquid asset to meet their financial obligation, such as paying supplier and employee on clock. By maintaining a positive cash flow, entrepreneurs can avoid financial difficulty and maintain a healthy business procedure. On the other paw, inadequate cash flow can lead to cash flow problem, which can hinder the growth and even lead to the ruination of a business. Entrepreneurs need to implement effective cash flow management strategy, such as maintaining a cash stockpile, optimizing cash collecting, and manage expense effectively. In plus to budget and cash flow management, entrepreneurs also need to have a thorough understanding of financial statements. Financial statements, such as the income statement, equilibrium shroud, and cash flow statement, provide valuable insight into the financial wellness and execution of a business. By analyzing these statements, entrepreneurs can assess their profitability, liquidity, and overall financial stance. Financial statements also help entrepreneurs evaluate the potency of their business strategy and make informed decisions about future investment and enlargement plan. Entrepreneurs should be familiar with key financial ratios, such as the current ratio, rejoin on investing, and debt-to-equity ratio. These ratios provide a snap of a business's financial execution and help entrepreneurs assess its profitability, liquidity, and solvency. By regularly analyzing these ratios, entrepreneurs can identify areas of betterment and take timely action to address any financial issue. Entrepreneurs should consider seeking professional financial advice. While entrepreneurs may possess a certain tier of financial cognition, it is always beneficial to consult with a financial adept to gain a fresh view and ensure that their financial decisions adjust with their business goal. A financial adviser can provide valuable insight, offer direction on financial plan and danger management, and help entrepreneurs make well-informed decisions about funding option and investing opportunity. Entrepreneurs need to stay informed about the latest financial trends and development in their industry. The financial landscape is constantly evolving, and entrepreneurs need to adapt to these change to stay ahead of the competitor. By staying abreast of industry trends, entrepreneurs can identify potential opportunity, palliate risk, and make proactive decisions that will positively impact the financial success of their business. Financial management is a critical aspect of running a successful business. By understanding and applying fundamental financial principle, entrepreneurs can effectively manage their money and achieve sustainable growth. Budget, cash flow management, understanding financial statements, analyzing financial ratios, seeking professional advice, and staying informed about industry trends are all crucial for entrepreneurs looking to grow their business and achieve long-term financial success.

XIII. FINANCIAL PLANNING FOR GROWTH AND EXPANSION

As entrepreneurs strive to take their businesses to the next tier, it becomes essential to carefully consider and plan for the financial implications of such growth. One of the first step in this procedure is to assess the potential costs associated with expansion, including hiring additional faculty, investing in substructure, and acquiring new equipment or technology. By estimating these expenses accurately, entrepreneurs can determine the sum of additional financing or funding they might need to secure to support their growth plans. This estimate can be done by conducting marketplace inquiry, consulting with manufacture expert, or engaging financial professional who specialize in helping businesses plan for growth. Once the potential costs have been identified, entrepreneurs must then explore various option to fund their growth and expansion. This can involve a combining of internal resources, such as reinvesting profit, using personal saving, or seeking financial supporting from friend and kinfolk. In many case, these internal resources may not be sufficient to cover the full extent of the expansion. In such situation, entrepreneurs may turn to external financing sources, such as loan from bank or financial institution, adventure uppercase investments, or administration grant or subsidy. Each financing source has its own advantage and disadvantage, and entrepreneurs must carefully evaluate which alternative align best with their growth objective, risk appetite, and long-term sustainability. As component of their financial planning for growth and expansion, entrepreneurs must also consider the potential impact on their cash flow. Expanding a business often requires significant upfront investments, which may result in temporary cash outflow. Entrepreneurs must ensure that they have sufficient liquid to cover these expenses, without jeopardizing their day-to-day operation or compromising their power to meet other financial obligation, such as paying supplier or employee. This requires monitor and manages cash flow projection, understanding the time of cash inflow and outflow, and implementing strategies to bridge any potential cash gap. In plus to the short-term impact on cash flow, entrepreneurs must also consider the long-term financial implications of their growth and expansion plans. This includes forecast and evaluating the potential return on investment (ROI) of the expansion, analyzing the impact on profitability, and assessing the overall financial feasibility of the growth scheme. Financial ratio, such as return on asset (ROA) , return on fairness (ROE) , and profits leeway, can be useful tool to assess the financial wellness and sustainability of the business before and after the expansion. It is important for entrepreneurs to conduct thorough financial psychoanalysis to ensure that the potential benefit of growth outweigh the associated costs and risks. Financial planning for growth and expansion should also involve eventuality planning and risk management. Entrepreneurs must anticipate potential challenge and setback that may arise during the expansion procedure and develop strategies to mitigate these risks. This can include measure such as diversifying receipts stream, construction strong relationship with supplier and customer, or implementing effective cost command measures. By proactively addressing these risks, entrepreneurs can protect their financial constancy and ensure the long-term achiever of their businesses. Financial planning for growth and expansion is a critical element of successful business management for entrepreneurs. By accurately assessing the potential costs, exploring financing option, monitoring cash flow, evaluating financial feasibility, and implementing risk management strategies, entrepreneurs can effectively plan for and navigate the financial challenge of growth. This allows them to seize opportunity, expand their businesses, and ultimately achieve their long-term goal and objective.

FINANCIAL PLANNING IN ACHIEVING BUSINESS GROWTH AND EXPANSION

The grandness of financial planning lie in its power to provide entrepreneurs with a systematic approach to managing their money and maximizing their resources. Effective financial planning enables entrepreneurs to make informed decisions regarding investment, cash flow management, and overall business performance. By carefully analyzing financial information and forecasting next trend, entrepreneurs can identify potential risks and opportunities, which in turning allows them to develop strategies to mitigate risks and capitalize on opportunities. Financial planning also helps entrepreneurs in setting realistic and achievable goal, as well as in creating a roadmap for the future growth and expansion of their businesses. One key aspect of financial planning is investing management. Entrepreneurs often face to gainsay of allocating their limited financial resources efficiently to generate maximum return. Right financial planning helps entrepreneurs in evaluating different investing opportunities and choosing the one that align with their business objective. By conducting thorough inquiry and psychoanalysis, entrepreneurs can identify investment that have the potential to generate high return, while also considering factor such as risk permissiveness and liquid need. This enables entrepreneurs to make informed decisions and avoid potential investing pitfall, ultimately leading to business growth and expansion. Another crucial aspect of financial planning is cash flow management. Cash flow is the lifeblood of any business, and efficient cash flow management is essential for its endurance and growth. By forecasting cash inflow and outflow, entrepreneurs can ensure that their businesses have sufficient liquid to meet their operational and financial obligation. Financial planning allows entrepreneurs to assess their cash need accurately and plan for any potential cash shortfall. It helps in identifying opportunities to optimize cash flow by implementing strategies such as managing account receivable and payable, negotiating favorable payment term with supplier, or improving inventorying management. By effectively managing their cash flow, entrepreneurs can ensure the smooth function of their businesses, seize growth opportunities, and expand their operation. Financial planning also plays a crucial part in monitoring and evaluating business performance. By using financial ratio, key performance indicator (KPIs) , and other financial tool, entrepreneurs can assess the financial wellness of their businesses and measure their progression towards achieving their goal. Financial planning enables entrepreneurs to monitor key metric such as profitability, liquid, solvency, and efficiency, which are essential for identifying area of betterment and making informed decisions to drive business growth. Financial planning helps in comparing actual outcome with the budgeted target, allowing entrepreneurs to identify deviation and take corrective action promptly. By regularly review and analyzing financial information, entrepreneurs can gain valuable insight into their business's performance, make necessary adjustment to their strategies, and ensure that their businesses are on racetrack to achieve growth and expansion. Financial planning is of overriding grandness for entrepreneurs aiming to achieve business growth and expansion. It provides them with a structured approach to managing their money, making informed investing decisions, optimizing cash flow, and monitoring and evaluating business performance. By incorporating financial planning into their business strategies, entrepreneurs can effectively allocate their resources, mitigate potential risks, capitalize on opportunities, and set realistic goal for the next. In doing so, they can lay the groundwork for long-term achiever and ensure sustainable growth and expansion of their businesses.

STRATEGIES FOR CREATING A FINANCIAL PLAN TO SUPPORT GROWTH INITIATIVES

Without a solid financial plan, entrepreneurs may find themselves unable to effectively manage their money or make informed decisions about their business. There are several strategies that entrepreneurs can utilize to create a financial plan that will support their growth initiatives. First and foremost, it is essential to accurately assess the current financial position of the business. This involves analyzing financial statement, such as the equilibrium shroud, income statement, and cash flow statement, to determine the current asset, liability, and cash flow of the business. By understanding the current financial position, entrepreneurs can identify any area of potency or helplessness and develop a plan to address them. Additionally, it is important to set clear financial goals and objective for the business. These goals should be realistic, measurable, and aligned with the overall growth scheme of the business. If the goal is to increase receipts by 20 % in the next year, the financial plan should outline the specific action and resource required to achieve this goal. It is also crucial to consider the timing and sequence of growth initiatives when creating a financial plan. Some growth initiatives may require significant upfront investment, such as expanding into new market or launching new product. Entrepreneurs should carefully consider the timing of these initiatives and ensure that they have the necessary financial resource to support them. This may involve securing additional financing through source such as investor, loan, or grant. Another scheme for creating a financial plan to support growth initiatives is to develop a cash flow forecast. A cash flow forecast project future cash inflow and outflow based on the expected timing and amount of receipts and expense. By creating a cash flow forecast, entrepreneurs can anticipate any potential cash shortfall and take proactive measure to address them. If the forecast indicates a cash shortage in three months, the entrepreneur may decide to reduce cost, postponement certain expense, or explore funding option to bridge the break. This allows the business to effectively manage its cash flow and ensure it has the necessary liquid to support its growth initiatives. It is important to regularly supervise and review the financial plan to ensure its potency. A financial plan is not a one-time exercising but a dynamic instrument that should be revised and updated as the business evolve. By regularly reviewing the financial plan, entrepreneurs can identify any variance or gap between the projected and actual outcome. This enables them to make informed adjustment to their financial scheme and ensure the plan remains aligned with the business's growth initiatives. Creating a financial plan that supports growth initiatives is crucial for the achiever of any business. By accurately assessing the current financial position, setting clear goals and objective, considering the timing of growth initiatives, developing a cash flow forecast, and regularly monitor and reviewing the plan, entrepreneurs can effectively manage their money and make informed decisions about their business's growth. By implementing this strategy, entrepreneurs can position their business for long-term achiever and achieve their growth objective.

TECHNIQUES FOR MONITORING AND ADJUSTING FINANCIAL PLANS AS THE BUSINESS EVOLVES

As entrepreneurs make strategic decisions and navigate the ever-changing marketplace landscape, they must continuously assess their financial plans to ensure alliance with their business goal. One technique that entrepreneurs can employ for monitoring their financial plans is budgeting. Budgeting involves setting financial target, allocating resource, and tracking actual expenses and receipts. By regularly comparing actual performance against budgeted expectations, entrepreneurs can identify discrepancies or variance and take appropriate corrective actions. If actual expenses exceed the budgeted sum, adjustment can be made such as cutting discretionary expenditure or exploring cost-saving measure. Conversely, if actual receipts exceed expectations, entrepreneurs can reassess their profits margin, search enlargement opportunity, or consider using surplus fund for investing. Another technique for monitoring financial plans is financial statement analysis. By examining financial statements such as the income statement, equilibrium shroud, and cash flowing statement, entrepreneurs can gain valuable insights into the financial wellness and performance of their business. Financial statement analysis involves analyzing key financial indicator and ratio to assess profitability, liquid, and solvency. For instance, entrepreneurs can calculate the gross profits leeway to evaluate the efficiency of their operation or the current proportion to assess their ability to meet short-term financial obligation. By regularly reviewing financial statements and comparing them to manufacture benchmark or historical information, entrepreneurs can identify any potential area of worry or area for betterment. Adjusting financial plans also involves adapting to changes in the business environment. One technique that entrepreneurs can employ in this respect is scenario analysis. Scenario analysis involves developing multiple financial scenarios based on different assumption or business conditions. By considering alternative scenarios, entrepreneurs can anticipate the potential impact of various event or circumstance on their financial plans. If a business operates in a highly volatile manufacture, entrepreneurs can develop scenarios for both optimistic and pessimistic marketplace conditions. By doing so, entrepreneurs can assess their business's resilience and financial viability under different scenarios, thereby enabling them to make informed decisions and develop eventuality plans. Additionally, entrepreneurs can use sensitivity analysis to evaluate the sensitivity of their financial plans to changes in key variable. Sensitivity analysis involves determining the impact of varying one fundamental varying while keeping other assumption constant. For instance, entrepreneurs can assess the impact of different concern rates, interchange rates, or sale volume on their financial plans. By conducting sensitivity analysis, entrepreneurs can identify the most significant driver of their financial performance and take appropriate actions to mitigate risk or exploit opportunity. Monitoring and adjusting financial plans is essential for entrepreneurs as their business evolve. Technique such as budget, financial statement analysis, scenario analysis, and sensitivity analysis can provide entrepreneurs with valuable insights and enable them to make informed decisions. By diligently monitoring their financial plans, entrepreneurs can identify discrepancies, assess their financial performance, and take corrective actions. By adapting their financial plans to changes in the business environment, entrepreneurs can enhance their business's resilience and financial viability. Effective monitoring and adjusting of financial plans contribute to the long-term achiever and increase of a business. Finance is a critical facet of managing a business. Successful entrepreneurs understand the importance of effectively managing their money in ordering to support growth and sustainability. This test explores fundamental financial principle that entrepreneurs should be aware of and provides insight on how to apply them to their business. One of the key principle entrepreneurs should understand is cash flow management. Cash flow is the lifeblood of a business and refers to the drift of money in and out of the business. It is important for entrepreneurs to monitor cash flow closely to ensure that they have enough liquid to meet their operational and financial obligation. This can be achieved by creating a cash flow forecast, which involves estimating the next inflows and outflow of cash. By analyzing this forecast, entrepreneurs can identify potential cash shortage and take appropriate action to mitigate them, such as securing additional funding or negotiating extended payment term with supplier. In plus to cash flow management, entrepreneurs should also focus on profitability. Profitability refers to the ability of a business to generate profit, which is crucial for its long-term success. Entrepreneurs can enhance profitability by closely monitoring their revenue and expenses, and implementing price command measures. It is important for entrepreneurs to regularly review their price scheme to ensure that it is competitive and aligned with the valuate they offer. Entrepreneurs should scrutinize their expenses and identify areas where they can reduce cost without compromising the caliber or efficiency of their product or service. By enhancing profitability, entrepreneurs can improve their business's financial performance and create a solid foundation for growth. Another financial precept entrepreneurs should consider is investment decision-making. Entrepreneurs often face investment decision, such as whether to purchase new equipment or expand their facility. These decision can have a significant effect on the financial health and growth possible of the business. It is important for entrepreneurs to carefully analyze the expected rejoin on investment (ROI) and weigh it against the associated risk. This can be achieved by estimating the cash inflows and outflow associated with the investment and discounting them to determine the net introduce valuate (NPV). If the NPV is positive, it indicates that the investment is expected to generate a rejoin higher than the price of uppercase and is thus financially viable. If the NPV is negative, entrepreneurs should reconsider the investment or explore alternative option. Entrepreneurs should be aware of the importance of financial statements in managing their business. Financial statements provide a snap of the business's financial performance and stance, and enable entrepreneurs to make informed decision. The most common financial statements include the income statement, balance sheet, and cash flow statement. The income statement provides information on the revenue, expenses, and net income of the business over a point of time. The balance sheet provides information on the asset, liability, and fairness of the business at a specific level in time. The cash flow statement provides information on the cash flows from operational, invest, and funding activity. By regularly review and analyzing these financial statements, entrepreneurs can gain insight into their business's financial health and identify areas where improvement can be made. Understanding fundamental financial principle and applying them to their business is essential for entrepreneurs to effectively manage their money and support growth. By focusing on cash flow management, profitability, investment decision-making, and financial statements, entrepreneurs can make informed financial decision and create a solid foundation for their business's success.

XIV. EXIT STRATEGIES AND SUCCESSION PLANNING

An exit strategy refers to a planned and organized way for an entrepreneur to leave a business they have founded or invested in. It outlines the step and action needed for a smooth transition of ownership or command. On the other hand, succession planning focuses on the continuance of the business beyond the entrepreneur's participation, ensuring its long-term viability and success. Both exit strategies and succession planning are crucial for entrepreneurs to consider, as they provide the model for future transition and safeguard the financial interests of the business and its stakeholder. One common exit strategy for entrepreneurs is selling the business. This option can be quite lucrative if the business has seen significant growth and has a favorable marketplace stance. To maximize to valuate of the business and attract potential buyers, entrepreneurs should focus on building up tangible and intangible assets. Tangible assets, such as real demesne and equipment, can be attractive to buyers looking for a turnkey operation. Intangible assets, such as brand mark repute, client ground, and intellectual belongings, also play a crucial part in determining the business's valuate. When selling a business, it is important for entrepreneurs to consider the time of the sale, marketplace weather, and potential buyers. Engaging the service of a business agent or investing banker can help navigate the complex procedure and ensure a smooth dealing. Another exit strategy is through an amalgamation or acquirement. This option involves combining the entrepreneur's business with another party or being acquired by a larger organization. Merger and acquisition offer several benefits, including admittance to new market, increased resource, and economy of surmount. The entrepreneur can negotiate a favorable bargain that provides financial protection and growth opportunity. This option requires careful circumstance and due industriousness to ensure compatibility with the acquiring party and alliance of value and goal. For those entrepreneurs who wish to retain some participation in the business but transfer ownership or command, the option of an employee buyout or management buyout may be suitable. In an employee buyout, the entrepreneur sells the business to employee. This option can provide persistence and constancy, as employee are familiar with the operations and can preserve the business's civilization and value. A management buyout, on the other hand, involves selling the business to current manager. This option allows the entrepreneur to entrust the business to individual who are already knowledgeable about its operations and have demonstrated leadership skill. Both employee buyouts and management buyouts require thorough planning, including financial arrangement, legal consideration, and ensuring a smooth transition of role and responsibility. Succession planning is equally important for entrepreneurs to ensure the long-term viability of their business. It involves identifying and preparing suitable successor to take over key leadership position within the organization. This procedure includes analyzing the current endowment pond, developing leadership and management skill, and creating a clear succession plan. Succession planning is not limited to the entrepreneur's immediate exit but should be an ongoing procedure to address potential contingency and development. By fostering a civilization of continuous learn and developing, entrepreneurs can ensure a smooth transition of leadership and maintain the business's competitive boundary. Exit strategies and succession planning are vital consideration for entrepreneurs to safeguard their financial interests and ensure the long-term viability of their business. Whether through selling the business, merging or acquiring, or engaging in employee buyouts or management buyouts, entrepreneurs have various option to transition out of their business successfully. Likewise, succession planning is crucial to identify and develop future leaders within the organization, ensuring its continued growth and success. By understanding the grandness of these strategies and implementing them effectively, entrepreneurs can pave the way for a successful transition and leave a lasting bequest.

EXIT STRATEGIES FOR ENTREPRENEURS

In the ever-changing world of business, entrepreneurs must be prepared for all possible outcome, including the need for an exit strategy. An exit strategy refer to the program an entrepreneur has in place to sell or liquidate their business should the need arise. While it may seem counterintuitive to think about ending a business venture before it even begins, having a well-thought-out exit strategy is of utmost grandness. Firstly, an exit strategy provides entrepreneurs with a clear roadmap on how to achieve their personal and financial goals. By having a predetermined program, entrepreneurs can better align their action and decision with their long-term objective. If an entrepreneur wish to retire by a certain year, having an exit strategy allows them to plan accordingly and ensure they have sufficient fund and resource to do so. An exit strategy serves as a safe earning for entrepreneurs should unexpected circumstances arise. Economical downturn, manufacture disruption, or personal reason may necessitate the need for a hasty exit. Without a well-defined exit strategy, entrepreneurs may find themselves overwhelmed and ill-prepared to navigate this challenge. On the other paw, by having an exit strategy in place, entrepreneurs can quickly make informed decision and minimize the negative effect on their personal and financial well-being. Additionally, having an exit strategy in place can increase an entrepreneur's believability and attractiveness to potential investors. Investors are more likely to invest in a business that has a well-thought-out exit strategy, as it demonstrates that the entrepreneur has thoroughly considered the risk and reward associated with their venture. It also indicates that the entrepreneur is committed to creating value and generating return, both for themselves and their investors. Thus, having an exit strategy in place can help entrepreneurs secure the necessary financing and supporting to grow their business and achieve their long-term goals. An exit strategy serves as an instrument for entrepreneurs to assess the value and attractiveness of their business to potential buyer or investors. By periodically reviewing and updating their exit strategy, entrepreneurs can identify area for betterment and take proactive measure to increase their business's value. This may include investing in key increase initiative, strengthening their intellectual belongings' portfolio, or streamlining operation to enhance profitability. By continuously evaluating and refining their exit strategy, entrepreneurs can stanch their business to achieve a higher evaluation and increase their likeliness of a successful exit. An exit strategy provides entrepreneurs with peace of mind and a sense of control over their business's future. Edifice and growing a business is an arduous and often stressful journeying. Having an exit strategy in place reassure entrepreneurs that they have a planned elude path should the need arise. This can alleviate some of the strain and anxiousness associated with entrepreneurship and allow entrepreneurs to focus more on the present and less on an uncertain future. While it may be uncomfortable to think about the ending of a business venture, having an exit strategy is crucial for entrepreneurs. It provides a clear roadmap to achieve personal and financial goals, prepares entrepreneurs for unexpected circumstances, increase believability with investors, assesses the value of the business, and provides peace of mind and a sense of control. By recognizing the grandness of exit strategy, entrepreneurs can better manage their financial resource and navigate the complex world of business with trust and resiliency.

TYPES OF EXIT STRATEGIES AVAILABLE: SELL THE BUSINESS, PASSING IT ON TO FAMILY, GOING PUBLIC, ETC.

One of the key decision that entrepreneurs have to make is determining the best exit strategy for their business. There are several types of exit strategy available, each with its own advantages and disadvantage. One option is selling the business, which involves finding a purchaser who is willing to take over the operation and asset of the company. This can be a preferred selection for entrepreneurs who are looking to cash out on their investing and move on to new venture or withdraw. Selling the business can provide a significant financial return if the company is successful and profitable. Finding the right purchaser can be a challenging and time-consuming procedure, and there is no assure of finding a purchaser at a desired cost. Another exit strategy is passing the business on to family members. This option allows the entrepreneur to keep the business within the family and potentially provide opportunity for future generation. It can also provide a feel of persistence and preserve the entrepreneur's bequest. This option may not be suitable if there are no suitable family members who are willing or capable of taking over the business. In plus, conflict and dispute may arise within the family regarding the possession and direction of the business, which can complicate the sequence procedure. Going public is another exit strategy that involves transforming the business into a publicly traded company by selling share of inventory to the public through an initial public offer (IPO) . This option allows entrepreneurs to admittance a large pond of uppercase and provide liquid to shareholders. Going public can also enhance the company's profile and repute, making it easier to attract customer and partner. The procedure of going public can be complex and expensive, requiring significant regulatory compliance and ongoing reportage requirement. The entrepreneur may lose command over the business if the bulk of the share are owned by public shareholders. Another exit strategy is merging with or acquiring another company. This option involves combining two or more company to create a larger and more competitive entity. Merger and acquisitions can provide synergy and economy of surmount by combining resource, capability, and client base. It can also provide a chance to diversify the business and enter new market. Merger and acquisitions can be highly complex and require careful due industriousness to ensure compatibility between the company. They may also result in organizational civilization clash and integrating challenge. Another exit strategy is elimination, which involves winding down the business and selling its asset in ordering to pay off debt and distribute any remaining fund to the entrepreneur. This option is often chosen when the business is no longer profitable or viable, or when the entrepreneur wants to retire or pursue other opportunity. Extermination can provide a quick and efficient path to exit the business, but it may result in a lower financial return and departure of the entrepreneur's investing. Entrepreneurs have several options for exiting their business, including selling the business, passing it on to family members, going public, merging with or acquiring another company, and elimination. Each of this strategy has its own advantages and disadvantage, and the selection of the best strategy depends on factor such as the entrepreneur's financial goal, personal preference, and the characteristic of the business. It is important for entrepreneurs to carefully evaluate each option and seek pro advice to make an informed determination that maximizes their financial return and ensures a smooth changeover.

SUCCESSION PLANNING IN ENSURING A SMOOTH TRANSITION OF THE BUSINESS TO NEW LEADERSHIP

Succession planning is the procedure of identifying and developing potential successor to take over key leadership position within the party when the current leaders step down or retire. It is an essential strategic instrument that allows for a smooth transition of the business to new leadership. Without proper succession planning, a business may face an innumerable of challenges and risks that could jeopardize its operation and future increase. One of the primary reason why succession planning is significant is that it minimizes disruption to business operation during the leadership transition point. When a key leader or administrator depart, there is often a temporary vacuum created in terms of decision-making and strategic way. With a well-thought-out succession plan in spot, the business can continue to function seamlessly as the new leader step into their part. This ensures that business strategy are carried forward and that employees, customer, and stakeholder experience minimal disruption. Consequently, the business is able to maintain its competitive vantage and preserve its marketplace deal, which is crucial in now's fast-paced and dynamic business environment. In addition to reducing disruption, effective succession planning also enables businesses to retain institutional knowledge and expertness. Over the path of their incumbency, leaders accumulate a significant sum of knowledge and insight that are vital to the success of the business. When these leaders depart without a clearly defined succession plan, there is a risk of losing this valuable intellectual uppercase. By identifying and developing potential successor, businesses can ensure a smooth transition of this knowledge, ensuring that the new leaders are adequately equipped to make informed decision and navigate the challenges of the manufacture. This not only enhances the constancy and persistence of the business but also facilitates its continued increase and invention. Succession planning plays a crucial part in maintaining employee morale and motivating. When employees see a clear vocation progress route within the establishment, they are more likely to be engaged and committed to their operate. Succession planning provides employees with the chance to develop their skill and capability, knowing that they have the potential to ascend to direction position in the next. This motivates them to perform at their best and fosters a positive operate environment. Additionally, when employees see their colleague being promoted internally, it instills a feel of trust and allegiance, thereby reducing upset rate and the associated cost of enlisting and preparation. Effective succession planning also mitigates the risks associated with external hiring. When a business is forced to find a replacing for a key leadership stance externally, it not only incurs substantial enlisting cost but also faces the challenge of finding somebody with the correct skill, feel, and cultural accommodate. In counterpoint, succession planning allows businesses to groom internal endowment who are already familiar with the establishment's civilization, value, and operation. This significantly reduces the clock and cost required for onboarding, while ensuring a smoother integrating into the business. Additionally, internal successor are more likely to have a deep understand of the business's unique challenges and objective, allowing them to hit the soil running and accelerate the tempo of decision-making. Succession planning is of utmost meaning in ensuring a smooth transition of the business to new leadership. It minimizes disruption, retains institutional knowledge, motivates employees, and mitigates the risks associated with external hiring. Entrepreneur must recognize the grandness of succession planning and invest the necessary clock, resource, and attempt into developing a comp and effective succession plan. By doing so, they can ensure the long-term success and sustainability of their businesses in an increasingly competitive and dynamic business landscape. Finance is a critical facet of any entrepreneurial adventure, as it presents entrepreneurs with a range of financial decisions that can significantly impact the growth and achiever of their business. To effectively manage their money and nurture business growth, entrepreneurs must possess a solid understanding of fundamental financial principle and know how to apply them. One such principle is budgeting, which entails estimate and allocating resources in a way that meets the business's need while ensuring financial stability and profitability. By developing a detailed budget, entrepreneurs can identify their sources of receipts and expense, assess their cash flow, and make informed decisions about the allotment of resources. Additionally, budgeting helps entrepreneurs set target and monitor their progression, enabling them to adjust their strategy accordingly. Another critical financial principle is cash flow direction. Cash flow refer to the drift of fund in and out of a business, and effectively managing it is vital for both short-term endurance and long-term growth. Entrepreneurs should carefully track their cash inflow and outflow, ensuring that there is a positive cash flow to cover expense and maintain a healthy financial standing. To manage cash flow effectively, entrepreneurs can implement various strategy, such as negotiating favorable payment term with supplier, incentivizing early payment from customer, and maintaining adequate cash reserve. Regularly monitor and analyzing cash flow statement can provide entrepreneurs with valuable insights into the financial wellness of their business, allowing them to identify potential risks or opportunity. Financial analysis is another indispensable instrument for entrepreneurs to manage their money and grow their business. By conducting a thorough analysis of their financial statement, entrepreneurs can gain a comprehensive understanding of their business's financial performance and make informed decisions. Financial analysis involves various techniques, such as proportion analysis, vogue analysis, and benchmarking, which provides entrepreneurs with insights into their profitability, liquid, efficiency, and solvency. By understanding these financial ratio and indicator, entrepreneurs can identify area of potency and helplessness, enabling them to focus their resources on improving performance and maximizing profitability. Additionally, understanding and managing the conception of risk is crucial for entrepreneurs in their financial decision-making procedure. Every business adventure carries inherent risks, and entrepreneurs must assess and mitigate these risks to protect their financial resources and ensure business sustainability. Risk direction involves identifying potential risks, evaluating their likeliness and affect, and implementing strategy to either transferal, palliate, or accept them. Entrepreneurs can employ various risk direction techniques, such as variegation, indemnity, and eventuality plan, to minimize the potential negative consequence of unforeseen event. By effectively managing risk, entrepreneurs can safeguard their financial resources and maintain financial stability in to confront of uncertainty. Entrepreneurs must also consider the financing options available to them and choose the most appropriate one for their business's unique need. There are various sources of financing, including personal saving, loan from financial institution, adventure capital, angel investor, crowdfunding, and grant. Each source has its advantage and disadvantage, and entrepreneurs must carefully evaluate their options based on factor such as the price of capital, refund term, command, and dilution of possession. By selecting the most suitable financing option, entrepreneurs can secure the necessary fund to start or expand their business, while minimizing financial stress and maximizing long-term growth potential. Understanding and applying fundamental financial principle are essential for entrepreneurs to effectively manage their money and grow their business. By budgeting, managing cash flow, conducting financial analysis, managing risk, and selecting appropriate financing options, entrepreneurs can make informed financial decisions that drive business growth and ensure its sustainability. By cultivating this financial frightfulness and continually adapting to changing marketplace weather, entrepreneurs can navigate the complex financial landscape and seize opportunity for achiever.

XV. ETHICAL CONSIDERATIONS IN FINANCIAL MANAGEMENT

As entrepreneurs navigate the complex terrain of financial management, it is important for them to consider the ethical implications of their decisions. In the chase of maximizing profit and growing their business, entrepreneurs must be aware of the potential impact their choice may have on various stakeholders. One of the fundamental ethical considerations in financial management is ensuring fair and transparent financial reportage. Precise and timely reporting not only provides stakeholders with a clear photograph of the company's financial wellness but also maintains the trust and confidence of investors, creditor, and employee. Any effort to manipulate or misrepresent financial info is not only morally wrong but may also lead to legal consequence. Another ethical consideration in financial management is the belief of candor in compensation practices. Entrepreneurs must strive to establish a fair and equitable compensation scheme that aligns with the contribution of employee to the success of the business. This includes providing competitive wage and benefit, offering opportunity for accomplishment developing and progression, and establishing performance-based incentive. Discriminative practices, such as sexuality or race-based compensate disparity, not only violate ethical principles but can also damage the company's reputation and hinder its long-term increase prospect. Ethical financial management requires entrepreneurs to make responsible and sustainable investment decisions. Investing in environmentally friendly practices, renewable vitality source, and socially responsible project not only benefit the satellite and fellowship but also enhances the company's brand mark picture and attracts socially conscious customers. In counterpoint, investing in industry or activity that harm the surroundings or exploit vulnerable population can have severe ethical implications and lead to reputational harm. By prioritizing ethical investments, entrepreneurs can create a positive impact on the globe while simultaneously fostering long-term business success. Additionally, ethical considerations extend to the intervention of suppliers and partner. Entrepreneurs must uphold fair deal practices, ensure timely payment to vendor, and avoid exploiting their bargain force to detrimentally affect smaller suppliers. Edifice strong and transparent relationships with suppliers not only cultivates a feel of trust and collaboration but also promotes sustainable and ethical supplying string management. Entrepreneurs should avoid engaging in questionable business practices, such as graft or corruptness when dealing with partner or administration entity. Upholding high standard of unity and honesty in business dealing not only aligns with ethical principles but also protects the company's reputation and mitigates legal risk. Entrepreneurs should consider the social and economic impact of their financial decisions. By actively engaging with local community and supporting economic developing initiative, entrepreneurs can contribute positively to fellowship and foster long-term business success. This may involve supporting local charity, investing in employee preparation program, or partnering with local small business. Working towards the amelioration of fellowship not only aligns with ethical principles but also helps build strong relationships with customers, employee, and other stakeholders. Ethical considerations play a vital part in financial management for entrepreneurs. By prioritizing fair and transparent financial reportage, establishing fair compensation practices, making responsible investments, fostering ethical relationships with suppliers and partner, and considering the social and economic impact of their decisions, entrepreneurs can ensure that their financial management practices align with ethical principles. Not only does ethical financial management gain stakeholders, but it also contributes to long-term business success by maintaining the trust and confidence of investors, attracting socially conscious customers, and enhancing the company's reputation. Integrating morality into financial decision-making is not only the right matter to do but also serves as a groundwork for sustainable increase and success in the business globe.

ETHICAL BEHAVIOR IN FINANCIAL MANAGEMENT

Ethical behavior in financial management is of utmost grandness for entrepreneurs in order to build credibility, establish trust with stakeholders, and ensure the long-term sustainability of their businesses. Financial management encompasses various activity such as budget, invest, and reportage, all of which require ethical decision-making. By adhering to ethical standards, entrepreneurs can enhance their reputation, attract investors, and foster a positive working environment. First and foremost, ethical behavior in financial management helps entrepreneurs build credibility and establish trust with various stakeholders. In today's business landscape, trust is a vital plus that determines the achiever or loser of a business. By acting ethically and transparently, entrepreneurs can build strong relationships with their customers, suppliers, and employees. For instance, when company upholds ethical standards in their financial practices, customers are more likely to trust them with their personal information and payment transaction. This, in turning, can lead to increased customer allegiance and repetition business. Similarly, suppliers are more likely to engage in long-term partnership with ethical businesses, ensuring a steady supplying string and favorable term. Employees tend to feel more safe and motivated when they work for a party with a strong ethical model. This creates a positive work environment and reduces upset rate, ultimately benefiting the financial execution of the business. Secondly, ethical behavior in financial management is essential for attracting investors. Investors look for businesses that demonstrate sound financial practices, as this reduces the tier of risk associated with their investment. Entrepreneurs who prioritize ethical behavior in their financial decision-making can present themselves as trustworthy and reliable partner in the eye of potential investors. These investors are more likely to entrust their capital to businesses that align with their own ethical standards. Ethical financial management ensures that investors' fund are used responsibly, thereby minimizing the risk of fraud or allocation. By attracting investors with shared value, entrepreneurs can admittance valuable capital to fuel the increase and enlargement of their businesses. Ethical behavior in financial management contributes to the long-term sustainability of a business. Unethical financial practices can lead to severe consequence such as legal troubles, reputation harm, and financial unbalance. Compliancy with ethical standards, on the other paw, helps entrepreneurs avoid this pitfall and create a sustainable business modeling. For instance, by accurately reporting financial information and adhering to taxation regulation, entrepreneurs can prevent legal dispute and fine. Additionally, ethical financial management allows entrepreneurs to build a strong brand reputation, which is a valuable intangible plus in today's competitive market. Customers are increasingly conscious of ethical and sustainable business practices, and are more likely to support and recommend businesses that align with their value. By acting ethically, entrepreneurs can gain a competitive vantage and ensure the seniority of their business. Ethical behavior in financial management is crucial for entrepreneurs in order to build credibility, establish trust with stakeholders, and ensure the long-term sustainability of their businesses.

By acting ethically, entrepreneurs can build strong relationships with their customers, suppliers, and employees, enhancing their reputation and fostering a positive working environment. Ethical financial practices also attract investors who seek businesses with sound financial management strategy, while reducing the risk of fraud or allocation. Ethical behavior contributes to the long-term sustainability of a business by preventing legal troubles, preserving brand reputation, and meeting customer expectation. Entrepreneurs should prioritize ethical behavior in their financial decision-making to create flourishing and responsible businesses.

COMMON ETHICAL DILEMMAS FACED BY ENTREPRENEURS

One of the most challenging aspect of being an entrepreneur is navigating through various ethical dilemmas that originate in the path of running a business. These dilemmas can often pit the entrepreneur's value and moral grasp against their business interests. There are several common ethical dilemmas faced by entrepreneurs that require careful consideration and decision-making. Firstly, entrepreneurs often face the dilemma of balancing financial success with social obligation. In the chase of maximizing profit, entrepreneurs may be tempted to cut corner and engage in unethical practice such as exploiting toil or disregarding environmental regulation. Entrepreneurs also have an obligation towards their employee, customer, and the broad society. Balancing financial success with social obligation requires making difficult choice that prioritize ethical practice over short-term gains. Another common ethical dilemma faced by entrepreneurs is maintaining transparency and honesty in business dealings. In a competitive market, entrepreneurs may be tempted to exaggerate the benefit of their product or service, misrepresent financial info, or engage in deceptive merchandising practice. Such knavery can have severe consequence for the entrepreneur's reputation and long-term success. Entrepreneurs must prioritize honesty and transparency in their business dealings, even if it means losing out on short-term gains or facing manufacture squeeze. Additionally, entrepreneurs often face the dilemma of respecting intellectual property rights. In an era of rapid invention, entrepreneurs must navigate complex intellectual property law and regulation to protect their own idea and Creation while respecting the rights of others. This dilemma requires entrepreneurs to strike an equilibrium between invention and respecting existing intellectual property rights. Failure to do so can lead to legal consequence and damage to the entrepreneur's reputation. Another common ethical dilemma faced by entrepreneurs is managing conflicts of interest. Entrepreneurs often find themselves in situation where their personal or financial interests conflict with the interests of their business. For instance, an entrepreneur may be tempted to award contract to a kinfolk appendage or acquaintance, even if there are better option available. This dilemma requires entrepreneurs to make decision that prioritize the best interests of their business over personal relationship or financial gains. Failure to do so can lead to conflicts, distrust, and damage to the entrepreneur's reputation. Entrepreneurs often face the dilemma of maintaining privacy and data security. In the digital age, business collect and store large amount of personal data, which creates ethical responsibility towards protecting the privacy and security of this info. Entrepreneurs must take appropriate measure to safeguard client data and ensure that it is not misused or compromised. Failure to do so can lead to legal liability, departure of client confidence, and reputational damage. Entrepreneurs often face the dilemma of managing ethical dilemmas within their own organizations. Issue such as work molestation, favoritism, or unethical demeanor by employee can pose significant challenge for entrepreneurs. Ethical leader must set a timbre of integrity and ethical demeanor within their organizations, establish clear policy and procedure, and take prompting and appropriate activity when ethical violation occur. Failure to address such issue can lead to a toxic operate surroundings, high employee upset, and damage to the entrepreneur's reputation. Being an entrepreneur comes with a throng of ethical dilemmas that require careful consideration and decision-making. These dilemmas' requirement that entrepreneurs' equilibrium financial success with social obligation, maintain transparency and honesty, respect intellectual property, handle conflicts of interest, maintain privacy and data security, and manage ethical dilemmas within their organizations. By navigating these dilemmas with integrity and ethical opinion, entrepreneurs can build successful business that not only generate profit but also contribute positively to society.

STRATEGIES FOR MAINTAINING ETHICAL STANDARDS IN FINANCIAL DECISION-MAKING

Given the possible for monetary gain and the complexity of financial transactions, ethical dilemmas often arise in the kingdom of finance. Entrepreneurs can adopt various strategies to ensure that their financial decisions adjust with ethical standards and maintain the confidence of stakeholders. Firstly, entrepreneurs can establish a robust code of ethics that outlines the ethical principles and value that guide their financial decision-making processes. This code should emphasize the grandness of honesty, transparency, and candor in all financial transactions. By clearly communicating these standards to all employees and stakeholders, entrepreneurs can create a culture of ethical conduct that permeates all aspect of their business operation. In plus to a code of ethics, entrepreneurs can further enhance their commitment to ethical standards by implementing internal controls and procedure. Entrepreneurs should segregate financial responsibility to prevent a single person from having complete control over financial resource. This separatism of duty ensures that different individual independently verify financial transactions, reducing the danger of fraudulent activity. Implementing regular financial audit conducted by external auditor helps to verify the truth and dependability of financial report, thus reinforcing the commitment to ethical financial practice. Alongside these measure, entrepreneurs should instill a feel of ethical decision-making among their employees. By providing regular preparation and teaching on ethical principles and dilemmas, entrepreneurs can equip employees with the cognition and critical think skill necessary to make ethical financial decisions. This preparation should include scenario or lawsuit study that highlight ethical dilemmas in financial decision-making and guidebook employees on how to navigate such situation in an ethical way. Additionally, entrepreneurs should foster an surrounding that encourages open discussion about ethical issue. By promoting a culture of communicating and transparency, employees are more likely to seek guidance and study concern about potential ethical lapse in financial decision-making. To complement these strategies, entrepreneurs can prioritize stakeholder engagement and alliance of interest. By considering the impact of financial decisions on all stakeholders, entrepreneurs can avoid decisions that prioritize short-term gain over long-term sustainability and ethical concern. Engaging with stakeholders, such as customer, supplier, employees, and the local community, allows entrepreneurs to understand their need and concern better. This understand can help guide financial decisions that not only maximize profit but also consider the well-being and interest of all stakeholders. Entrepreneurs can integrate environmental, social, and governing (ESG) factor into their financial decision-making processes. By incorporating ESG criterion, entrepreneurs can align their financial decisions with broader societal goal, such as environmental sustainability and social obligation. This can be achieved by considering the environmental impact of business activity, prioritizing socially responsible investment, and adopting governing practice that ensure transparency and answerability. Entrepreneurs can seek external guidance and adhere to existing manufacture standards and regulations. By consulting with financial advisor, legal expert, and manufacture association, entrepreneurs can gain valuable insight into best practice and legal requirement for ethical financial decision-making. This external guidance can help entrepreneurs navigate complex financial issue and ensure compliance with relevant law and regulations. Maintaining ethical standards in financial decision-making is essential for entrepreneurs to build and sustain successful businesses. By implementing strategies such as establishing a code of ethics, implementing internal controls, training employees, prioritizing stakeholder engagement, integrating ESG factor, and seeking external guidance, entrepreneurs can ensure that their financial decisions uphold high ethical standards. Through these strategies, entrepreneurs can build a repute for ethical conduct that not only attracts stakeholders but also contributes to the long-term achiever and sustainability of their businesses. Despite having a great business thought, many entrepreneurs struggle with managing their finance effectively. Finance is a critical facet of any business, and understanding fundamental financial principles is essential for the success and growth of an entrepreneurial venture. One of the key principles entrepreneurs need to grasp is the concept of cash flow. Cash flow refer to the drift of money in and out of a business and is crucial for its day-to-day operation. By monitoring their cash flow, entrepreneurs can ensure that they have enough liquid to cover their expenses and seize opportunity for growth. They need to keep a close eyeball on their cash inflow, which include receipts from sale, investment, and loan, as well as their cash outflow, such as salary, lease, and purchase. Additionally, entrepreneurs should be mindful of the time of their cash flow, as delay in payment can pose challenge to meeting their financial obligation. Another essential financial principle for entrepreneurs to understand is profitability. Profitability measures the power of a business to generate a profit by comparing its receipts to its expenses. It is not sufficient for entrepreneurs to focus solely on receipts growth ; they must also monitor and control their expenses to ensure a healthy profits' leeway. By analyzing their profits and departure statement regularly, entrepreneurs can identify area where cost can be reduced or receipts can be increased. This information is crucial for making informed decisions and optimizing the financial performance of the business. Additionally, entrepreneurs should consider the concept of leverage when managing their finance. Leverage involves using borrowed uppercase to finance a business's operation or investment. While leverage can amplify profit, it also increases the danger to the business. Entrepreneurs must weigh the potential benefit of leverage against the associated risk and decide if it aligns with their business goal and danger permissiveness. It is also necessary for entrepreneurs to understand the grandness of budgeting and forecast in financial management. Creating a budget allows them to plan and allocate resource effectively. It involves estimating future revenue and expenses and setting financial target. By tracking their actual financial performance against the budget, entrepreneurs can identify deviation and take corrective action if necessary. In addition to budgeting, forecast is crucial for entrepreneurs as it helps them anticipate future financial outcome. By analyzing historical trend and marketplace weather, entrepreneurs can make informed projection about their cash flow, receipts, and expenses. This information enables them to make strategic decisions and adapt their business plan accordingly. Entrepreneurs should be aware of the financial tools and resource available to them. Engineering has revolutionized financial management, offering entrepreneurs a wide array of package application and platform to streamline their financial process. These tools can assist with accountancy, invoice, payroll, and financial reportage, saving entrepreneurs both clock and money. Entrepreneurs should also consider seeking professional advice. Accountant and financial advisor can provide direction on managing finance, taxation plan, and investing strategy. Their expertness can help entrepreneurs navigate the complexity of financial management and ensure compliance with regulatory requirement. Finance plays a vital part in the success and growth of an entrepreneurial venture. By understanding fundamental financial principles and how to apply them, entrepreneurs can effectively manage their money and grow their business. By monitoring cash flow, analyzing profitability, considering leverage, budgeting and forecast, and utilizing financial tools and professional advice, entrepreneurs can empower themselves to make informed decisions and secure the financial wellness and seniority of their business.

XVI. CONCLUSION

The financial aspect of running a business are critical to its success. Entrepreneurs must understand and apply fundamental financial principles in ordering to effectively manage their money and grow their business. Throughout this book, we have explored various key concepts and strategies that entrepreneurs can utilize to ensure financial sustainability. We have seen the importance of budgeting and cash flow management in maintaining liquid and make informed financial decisions. We have highlighted the meaning of financial statements in assessing a business's execution and attracting potential investor. Additionally, managing credit and debt is crucial to long-term financial constancy and growth. By effectively leveraging credit and carefully managing debt, entrepreneurs can admittance necessary fund and expand their operation. This book has emphasized the part of financial forecasting and plan in setting realistic goals and strategies for the next. By considering both short-term and long-term financial projection, entrepreneurs can make informed decisions that align with their business objectives. We have discussed the benefit of diversifying income source and utilizing various investing option to maximize return. By diversifying income stream, entrepreneurs can reduce their trust on a single receipts generator and minimize the effect of economic fluctuation. This book has highlighted the importance of financial literacy and seeking professional advice when needed. Entrepreneurs should continuously educate themselves on financial matter and operate closely with financial expert to improve their financial management skills. In doing so, they can navigate complex financial landscape and make informed decisions that align with their business goals. Financial management is a crucial facet of entrepreneurship that requires cognition, correction, and strategic plan. While it may seem daunting, mastering these financial principles is essential for long-term success. By implementing the strategies discussed in this book, entrepreneurs can effectively manage their money, navigate financial challenge, and fuel the growth of their businesses. As financial literacy and expertness remain to play a pivotal part in the entrepreneurial landscape, it is crucial for entrepreneurs to invest clock and attempt into developing their financial management skills. By doing so, they can stanch themselves for success and achieve their business objectives. Understanding and applying fundamental financial principles is not just essential for entrepreneurs, but for any individual looking to grow their riches and achieve financial protection. Whether it is managing personal finance or running a business, the principles of budgeting, cash flow management, financial statements, credit and debt management, financial forecasting, variegation, and seeking professional advice apply universally. By gaining a thorough understanding of these concepts and implementing them effectively, entrepreneurs can ensure the financial sustainability and growth of their businesses. Financial management is a critical element of entrepreneurship that requires continuous learning and adaption. It is through strategic financial plan and informed decision-making that entrepreneurs can build successful businesses and achieve their financial goals. As the globe of business continues to evolve, the importance of financial frightfulness will only increase, making it imperative for entrepreneurs to develop a strong groundwork in financial management. By doing so, they can unlock the full possible of their businesses and pave the path for long-term success.

RECAP OF THE MAIN POINTS DISCUSSED IN THE BOOK

In this book, we have explored the issue of finance for entrepreneurs and how they can effectively manage their money and grow their businesses. Several key points have been discussed throughout this slice, and it is important to recap this main highlight. First and foremost, it is essential for entrepreneurs to have a solid understand of basic financial principle. This means familiarizing themselves with concept such as cash flow management, budgeting, and financial statements. By grasping this fundamental concept, entrepreneurs can make informed decision about their business finances and take step to ensure profitability and long-term sustainability. Another crucial point that has been stressed is the importance of setting financial goals and creating a comprehensive financial plan. Entrepreneurs need to establish clear objective for their business and develop a roadmap to achieve those goals. This involves creating a budget that outlines projected revenue and expenses, as well as regularly review and adjusting the plan as necessary. By setting financial goals and creating a plan, entrepreneurs can stay focused and motivated, ensuring that their business's financial management align with their overall objective. Effective cash flow management has been highlighted as a key element in a business's financial success. Entrepreneurs must understand that cash flow is the lifeblood of their business and must be carefully monitored and managed. This includes keeping racetrack of cash inflow and outflow, minimizing expenses, and ensuring that there is enough liquid to cover short-term obligation.

By effectively managing cash flow, entrepreneurs can maintain financial constancy, meet financial obligation, and seize increase opportunity. Additionally, the importance of separating personal and business finances has been emphasized. Entrepreneurs should establish separate deposit account and recognition card for their business, ensuring that there is clear breakup between personal and business expenses. This not only helps with financial establishment but also provides legal security and allows for accurate financial reportage. By separating personal and business finances, entrepreneurs can better racetrack and manage their business's financial execution and avoid potential legal and taxation complication. This book has discussed the meaning of regularly monitor and analyzing financial statements. Financial statements, such as the income statement, equilibrium shroud, and cash flow statement, provide valuable insight into a business's financial wellness and execution. Entrepreneurs must review these statements on a regular fundament to identify area of betterment, assess profitability and liquid, and make informed decision. By analyzing financial statements, entrepreneurs can identify trend, spot potential issue, and adjust their financial management strategy accordingly. The book has touched upon the importance of seeking professional advice and utilizing financial tools and resources. Entrepreneurs should not hesitate to consult with accountant, financial advisor, or other expert who can provide direction and supporting. Additionally, there are various financial tools and resources available, such as accountancy package, budgeting apps, and online financial course, that can assist entrepreneurs in managing their money effectively. By leveraging these resources, entrepreneurs can enhance their financial cognition and skill, improving their overall financial management capability. This book has highlighted several key points for entrepreneurs to consider when managing their finances. By understanding basic financial principle, setting financial goals and creating a comprehensive plan, managing cash flow, separating personal and business finances, monitoring financial statements, and seeking professional advice and utilizing resources, entrepreneurs can effectively manage their money and grow their businesses. Financial management is a critical facet of entrepreneurship and by implementing these key points, entrepreneurs can stanch themselves for long-term success.

EMPHASIS ON THE IMPORTANCE OF FINANCIAL MANAGEMENT FOR ENTREPRENEURS

Effective financial management is the linchpin of any successful business, as it directly impacts the establishment's profitability, sustainability, and growth potential. In ordering to successfully manage their finances, entrepreneurs must have a deep understand of financial principles and know how to apply them to their business operation. One key cause why financial management is crucial for entrepreneurs is its direct effect on their business's profitability. By effectively managing their finances, entrepreneurs can identify the most profitable area of their operation and make informed decision to maximize their profits. For instance, through proper financial analysis, entrepreneurs can determine which product or service are generating the highest profit margin and allocate their resource accordingly. They can also identify cost-saving opportunities and make adjustment to their expenditure, which can significantly improve their bottom pipeline. By closely monitoring their financial position, entrepreneurs can identify potential financial risk or issue and take corrective action before they become detrimental to their profitability. Financial management plays a critical part in ensuring that entrepreneurs can maximize their profits and achieve long-term financial success. Financial management is vital for entrepreneurs because it directly influences the sustainability of their business. Entrepreneurs need to carefully manage their cash flow, which refers to the influx and leakage of money in their business. Without adequate financial management, entrepreneurs may face cash flow issue, such as running out of cash to pay for their expense or failing to collect payment from customer on clock. These cash flow problem can quickly lead to a crisis and even coerce entrepreneurs to shut down their business. By implementing effective financial management strategy, entrepreneurs can proactively address cash flow challenge. They can develop cash flow projection to anticipate their future financial need, implement payment collection processes to ensure timely reception of payment, and negotiate favorable term with supplier to manage their cash outflow effectively. By ensuring a healthy cash flow, entrepreneurs can maintain the sustainability of their business and sail through potential financial obstacle. In plus to profitability and sustainability, financial management is also crucial for entrepreneurs because it directly impacts their business's growth potential. Entrepreneurs need to make strategic financial decision that adjust with their growth objective and enable them to seize opportunities for enlargement. By effectively managing their finances, entrepreneurs can secure the necessary financing for growth initiative, whether it's through external funding, investment, or reinvesting their profits. They can also analyze their financial information to identify marketplace trend, client preference, and emerging opportunities, which can inform their strategic decision and enable them to capitalize on growth prospect. In counterpoint, poor financial management can hinder a business's growth potential, as it may lead to missed opportunities, inefficient resourcefulness allotment, or limited admittance to uppercase. Entrepreneurs must prioritize financial management to not only sustain their business but also unlock its full growth potential. Financial management is of utmost grandness for entrepreneurs. By understanding financial principles and applying them to their business operation, entrepreneurs can enhance their profitability, ensure the sustainability of their business, and unlock its growth potential. Whether it's through effective financial analysis, cash flow management, or strategic decision-making, entrepreneurs must prioritize financial management to navigate the complexity of the business globe and achieve long-term success. Financial management is a critical accomplishment for entrepreneurs seeking to manage their money wisely and grow their business.

ENCOURAGEMENT FOR ENTREPRENEURS TO APPLY THE PRINCIPLES LEARNED TO EFFECTIVELY MANAGE THEIR MONEY AND GROW THEIR BUSINESSES

It is very important for entrepreneurs to apply the financial principles they have learned to effectively manage their money and grow their businesses. By understanding the fundamental concept of finance, entrepreneurs can make informed decisions that will positively impact their business's success. Implementing proper financial plan and budget technique will allow entrepreneurs to allocate resource wisely and achieve their goal. Additionally, entrepreneurs must consider the various sources of financing available to them, such as loan, investment, or grant, to support their business increase initiative. By effectively managing their money, entrepreneurs can avoid common financial pitfall and ensure the long-term sustainability and profitability of their ventures. Entrepreneurs should continuously monitor and evaluate their financial performance to identify area for betterment and make necessary adjustment. This includes regularly assessing their cash flowing, profits and departure statement, and equilibrium sheet to maintain a clear understanding of their business's financial wellness. By doing so, entrepreneurs can make strategic decisions to optimize their resource and maximize their profitability. It is also crucial for entrepreneurs to establish strong financial accountability within their organization. This can be achieved by implementing reliable accountancy system and procedure that accurately track and report financial transaction. By maintaining transparency and accountability in financial matter, entrepreneurs can build confidence with stakeholder and attract potential investor or partner. Entrepreneurs must stay updated on the latest financial trends and regulatory change that may impact their business operations. This includes staying informed about taxation regulations, industry-specific financial practice, and emerging financing options. By having a deep understanding of the financial landscape, entrepreneurs can position themselves strategically and take vantage of new opportunity or mitigate potential risk. But certainly not least, entrepreneurs should seek professional direction when necessary. By consulting with financial advisor or expert, entrepreneurs can gain valuable insight and expertness that can assist them in making better financial decisions. These professionals can provide expert advice on taxation plan, financial danger appraisal, investing strategy, and overall business financial management. The cognition and insight gained from these professionals can be instrumental in ensuring the success and sustainability of the entrepreneur's venture. Finance is an essential facet of entrepreneurship that cannot be overlooked. By applying the principles learned throughout this path, entrepreneurs can effectively manage their money and grow their businesses. The ability to make informed financial decisions is a crucial accomplishment for entrepreneurs, and it can significantly impact the success of their ventures. By understanding the basics of finance, creating a solid financial program, exploring financing options, monitoring financial performance, establishing financial accountability, staying informed about trends and regulations, and seeking professional advice when necessary, entrepreneurs can position themselves for long-term success. Entrepreneurs

must recognize to valuate of financial management and make
it a precedence in their business operations.

BIBLIOGRAPHY

Entrepreneur magazine. 'e-Business.' Step-by-Step Startup Guide, Entrepreneur Press, 5/17/2014

Basil Peters. 'Early Exits.' Exit Strategies for Entrepreneurs and Angel Investors (but Maybe Not Venture Capitalists), Basil Peters, 1/1/2009

CA Ravi Mamodiya. 'Taxmann's Business Succession Planning – Explaining the Approach, Strategy & Execution in a Simplified Manner with the Help of Business Continuity Strategies, Practical Case Studies & Checklists.' Taxmann Publications Private Limited, 5/9/2023

Luna Z. Rainstorm. 'Flexible Budgeting Essentials.' A Route to Financial Success, Xspurts.com, 1/1/2023

Danny M Boyd. 'Small Beginnings, Big Results.' A Business Big Idea Guidebook to Financial Success, Amazon Digital Services LLC - Kdp, 5/15/2023

H. Oliver Welch. 'The History of Financial Planning.' The Transformation of Financial Services, E. Denby Brandon, Jr., John Wiley & Sons, 10/12/2009

Zaigham Mahmood. 'Software Project Management for Distributed Computing.' Life-Cycle Methods for Developing Scalable and Reliable Tools, Springer, 4/4/2017

Frank Bannister. 'Purchasing and Financial Management of Information Technology.' Routledge, 6/25/2012

Erich A. Helfert. 'Financial Analysis Tools and Techniques: A Guide for Managers.' McGraw Hill Professional, 11/20/2001

Adamu Idris Tanko. 'Prudence, Transparency and Accountability.' Proceedings of the Second National Conference on Ethical Issues in Accounting, Kabiru Isa Dandago, Gidan Dabino Publishers, 1/1/2004

M. F. VAN. BREDA. 'Towards a Definition of Financial Control Systems (Classic Reprint).' Fb&c Limited, 2/8/2018

United States Government Accountability Office. 'Standards for Internal Control in the Federal Government.' Lulu.com, 3/24/2019

Jody Blazek. 'Tax Planning and Compliance for Tax-Exempt Organizations.' Rules, Checklists, Procedures, Wiley, 1/4/2012

Jeffrey T. Craig. 'Personal Financial Planning for Executives and Entrepreneurs.' The Path to Financial Peace of Mind, Michael J. Nathanson, Springer Nature, 4/22/2021

Jody Blazek. 'Tax Planning and Compliance for Tax-Exempt Organizations.' Rules, Checklists, Procedures, 2021 Supplement, John Wiley & Sons, 4/20/2021

Anja Böhm. 'Interpretation of key figures in financial analysis.' GRIN Verlag, 9/11/2008

Axel Tracy. 'Ratio Analysis Fundamentals.' How 17 Financial Ratios Can Allow You to Analyse Any Business on the Planet, RatioAnalysis.net, 12/7/2012

René M. Stulz. 'The Risks of Financial Institutions.' Mark Carey, University of Chicago Press, 11/1/2007

Chiara Crovini. 'Risk Management in Small and Medium Enterprises.' Routledge, 2/13/2019

Scott Harrington. 'Risk Management and Insurance.' McGraw-Hill Companies,Incorporated, 7/15/2003

Patty Graybeal. 'Principles of Accounting Volume 2 - Managerial Accounting.' Mitchell Franklin, 12th Media Services, 2/14/2019

Marvin Namanda. 'Capital Budgeting, Net Present Value and other Business Decision Making Tools.' GRIN Verlag, 3/31/2017

Mike Simonetto. 'Pricing and Profitability Management.' A Practical Guide for Business Leaders, Julie Meehan, John Wiley & Sons, 6/28/2011

Edward J. Vanderbeck. 'Principles of Cost Accounting.' Cengage Learning, 2/1/2012

Robert S. Kaplan. 'Measure Costs Right.' Make the Right Decisions, Robin Cooper, Harvard Business Review, Reprint Service, 1/1/1988

Martin Fassnacht. 'Price Management.' Strategy, Analysis, Decision, Implementation, Hermann Simon, Springer, 12/11/2018

Jim Schell. 'Small Business For Dummies.' Eric Tyson, John Wiley & Sons, 11/30/2011

Garima Malik. 'Funding Options for Startups.' A Conceptual Framework and Practical Guide, K. S. V. Menon, Notion Press, 5/7/2016

Leo Kanell. 'The Business Funding Formula.' How Entrepreneurs Are Jumpstarting Their Businesses With Powerful Funding Strategies, Leo Kanell , 1/18/2017

Garry Stephenson. 'Whole Farm Management.' From Start-Up to Sustainability, Storey Publishing, 11/12/2019

Alan G. Seidner. 'Cash & Investment Management for Nonprofit Organizations.' John Zietlow, John Wiley & Sons, 4/10/2007

George T. Friedlob. 'Understanding Cash Flow.' Franklin J. Plewa, Jr., John Wiley & Sons, 1/1/1995

Peter B. Heyler. 'Managing Cash Flow.' An Operational Focus, Rob Reider, John Wiley & Sons, 2/17/2003

Steve Player. 'Future Ready.' How to Master Business Forecasting, Steve Morlidge, John Wiley & Sons, 2/19/2010

Christy Wright. 'Business Boutique.' A Woman's Guide for Making Money Doing What She Loves, Ramsey Press, 4/17/2017

Nigel Wyatt. 'The Financial Times Essential Guide to Budgeting and Forecasting.' How to Deliver Accurate Numbers, Pearson UK, 12/14/2012

Fernando Alvarez. 'Financial Statement Analysis.' A Practitioner's Guide, Martin S. Fridson, John Wiley & Sons, 4/19/2022

Mariusz Skonieczny. 'The Basics of Understanding Financial Statements.' Learn how to Read Financial Statements by Understanding the Balance Sheet, the Income Statement, and the Cash Flow Statement, Investment Publishing, 1/1/2012

Aileen Ormiston. 'Understanding Financial Statements.' Lyn M. Fraser, Pearson Education, 1/5/2015

Noam Wasserman. 'The Founder's Dilemmas.' Anticipating and Avoiding the Pitfalls That Can Sink a Startup, Princeton University Press, 4/1/2013

Jeffrey T. Craig. 'Personal Financial Planning for Executives and Entrepreneurs.' The Path to Financial Peace of Mind, Michael J. Nathanson, Springer, 11/12/2018

Donald F. Kuratko. 'Introduction to Entrepreneurship.' South-Western, 1/1/2009